THE FIRST PRINCIPLES

THE FIRST PRINCIPLES

By John Robert Stevens

LIVING WORD PUBLICATIONS

John Robert Stevens

From the day he preached his first sermon in 1933 at the age of fourteen, John Robert Stevens answered God's unique call upon his life. As a minister and teacher, he devoted his life to serving the Lord and His people. He was able, in a very simple way, to unlock the secrets of the Word of God and share them with hungry hearts. Today, many believers and churches are discovering the depth of his messages from The Living Word.

John Robert Stevens was first and foremost a minister of restoration, with the goal in mind of seeing the Church restored to its original purity and power. His ministry inspired the establishment of churches throughout the United States and around the world, known as "The Living Word Fellowship." A collection of more than 12,000 carefully recorded tapes and over 1,000 books, manuals, and pamphlets exists today as a source of John Robert Stevens' timeless teachings.

Author's Note

The purpose of this series of Bible studies is to lay the foundation of truth—the first principles of the oracles of God. These lessons are not intended to deal exhaustively with the fundamental truths of the Bible; they are a simple introduction to those great truths.

Each lesson is presented in brief outline form. I purposely did not elaborate on points presented in these outlines, because various churches, Bible classes, and individuals may not be at the same stage of spiritual development nor ready for the same depth of instruction.

While this series of Bible lessons is elementary in scope, Bible students will soon realize that many biblical truths that are taught here are beyond the scope of the average believer's experience.

The heart of the studies is the progressive revelation of the Scriptures to the believer. From the days of the Reformation until the present hour, the Church has witnessed a progressive unfolding of the Scriptures, until each generation of believers has entered into newly restored Bible experiences and understanding. It will continue to be so. Tomorrow's light will be brighter than today's; tomorrow's Church will be closer to the New Testament pattern for the Church than today's.

Our Lord expects no more or no less of us than this, that we be willing to seek and to walk in the light He is bringing forth to the hearts of men. Let us pray that our ears not be dull of hearing, nor our eyes dim that we cannot see. May we hear what God is speaking today, and may we see what He is doing in the earth in our times. Let us have faith without presumption. Let us search the Word daily to see whether these things be so (Acts 17:11). Blessed is he who has ears to hear what the Spirit is saying to the churches.

John Robert Stevens

Table of Contents

BREAD FOR THE LITTLE CHILDREN

MEAT FOR THE YOUNG MEN

For when by reason of the time ye ought to be teachers, ye have need again that some one teach you the rudiments of the first principles of the oracles of God; and are become such as have need of milk, and not of solid food. For every one that partaketh of milk is without experience of the word of righteousness; for he is a babe. But solid food is for fullgrown men, even those who by reason of use have their senses exercised to discern good and evil. Wherefore leaving the doctrine of the first principles of Christ, let us press on unto perfection.... And this will we do, if God permit.

Hebrews 5:12—6:3, ASV.

About The First Principles

The First Principles began as John Robert Stevens' outline of lessons used in the evangelistic field. Through revelation and prophecies of the Holy Spirit, the Lord directed the preparation of these 50 lessons. The goal was to present the lessons in a simple way so that they could be used effectively with Bible students of any level of maturity.

The First Principles is grouped into three major sections: "Milk for the Babes," "Bread for the Children," and "Meat for the Young Men." These sections are designed to address varying spiritual levels and stages of development (I John 2:1,12–14, 28–29 and I John 3:7). The scriptural principles presented in this manual build progressively from Lesson 1 to Lesson 50; however, you should feel free to study the lessons in an order which best applies to your spiritual level or current emphasis. The page layout includes wide margins to allow you to make notes.

These outlines are entirely based upon the Scriptures. In a few cases, specific Bible translations are quoted to enhance a point. However, use the Bible translations which are the most appropriate for you or your group. In some instances, entire chapters will be cited; in other cases, the lesson will refer to specific verses, shining the light of emphasis on just a verse or two. In a classroom situation, the teacher may wish to summarize lengthy passages rather than reading them aloud. When multiple Scriptures are cited for one point, all of the references shed light on one another. These verses are meant to be read in the order presented.

Suggested Applications of the Manual

Personal Devotions: *The First Principles* can be used as a resource for your personal devotional life. You can study the lessons at your own pace, research the Scripture verses, and benefit from a topical study of the Bible.

Group Bible Study: *The First Principles* can provide a framework for stimulating home study groups or classroom Bible studies. Prior to the meeting, students can read the lesson and study the Scripture verses. Then they can come together to discuss and share the passages and principles which were especially meaningful to them. A teacher may wish to have a student prepare a lesson in advance, reading the Scriptures and seeking the Lord as to how to lead the group. The responsibility of teaching can help the student attain a greater understanding of the lesson.

A teacher who is sensitive to the leading and anointing of the Holy Spirit can encourage participation, guide the discussions, and help lead people into actual experiences with the Lord based on the truths presented. The teacher should create an atmosphere that allows maximum individual participation, so that students can explore truths without restraint, while steering them away from misconceptions.

In-depth Research: For a deeper study of the Scriptures, *The First Principles* may be used as a starting point for in-depth research of major biblical themes. Using concordances, lexicons, and Bible software, the diligent student can look to the Scriptures for further examples and support of the basic principles outlined.

Sermon Outlines: With clearly outlined themes and listings of major points, *The First Principles* can serve as sermon outlines for teachers and ministers at all levels. Prayerful meditation on the teachings and Scriptures presented in the lessons, combined with waiting on the Lord, can open the door for the Holy Spirit to speak a true, living Word to the heart.

The publication of this edition of *The First Principles* has been undertaken with great care to create a manual that is not only true to the original goal but is also presented in language and content that is fresh and current for today's Bible students and scholars.

MILK
FOR THE
BABES

Salvation

SCRIPTURE READINGS

Genesis 2 and 3
John 3

LESSON

I. **God's command to the first man.**
    Genesis 2:16–17

II. **The first man disobeyed God's command.**
     This was the beginning of sin.
     Genesis 3:6

III. **The result of disobedience (or sin) to God.**
      Read Romans 6:23 with Genesis 3:16–24.

IV. **Who has sinned?**
     Isaiah 53:6   Romans 3:23   Romans 3:10–12

V. **Sin came upon us through one man; salvation from sin came also through one Man, Jesus Christ.**
    Romans 5:6–12,15–18

VI. **The payment for our sin was the blood of Jesus Christ.**
     Leviticus 17:11   Hebrews 9:22   Romans 5:8–9

VII. **How are my sins forgiven?**

    A. Repent.
        Luke 13:3–5

    B. Confess.
        I John 1:9

C. Receive Jesus.
John 1:12–13

D. Believe.
Acts 16:31

E. Come.
John 6:37

MEMORY VERSE

John 1:12

Jesus Christ, Our Savior

SCRIPTURE READINGS

Isaiah 53
John 6

LESSON

I.   **What did Jesus Christ do for us?**

   A.   He came to earth to be our Savior.
        Luke 2:11   John 3:17   I Timothy 1:15
        Hebrews 7:25

   B.   He was our substitute.
        Isaiah 53:5–6   Hebrews 2:9   I Peter 3:18

   C.   He was our sin-bearer.
        I Peter 2:24   Hebrews 9:28   Isaiah 53:12

II. **What does Jesus Christ do for us now?**

   A.   He is our burden-bearer.
        Matthew 11:28–30

   B.   He is our intercessor.
        Hebrews 7:25

   C.   He is our deliverer from perishing.
        John 3:14–15

   D.   He is the only food for our souls.
        John 6:35

   E.   He is our only source of truth.
        John 6:67–69

  F. He is our only Savior and deliverer.
    Acts 4:12

  G. He is our only foundation.
    I Corinthians 3:11

MEMORY VERSES

Matthew 11:28; Luke 19:10

Jesus Christ, Our Risen Lord

SCRIPTURE READINGS

I Corinthians 15   Luke 24
Matthew 28   John 20 and 21
Mark 16

LESSON

I.   **Jesus Christ rose from the dead.**

    A.   His resurrection was announced by angels.
        Matthew 28:6   Mark 16:6   Luke 24:6

    B.   His resurrection was witnessed by His disciples.
        Acts 3:14–15   Acts 4:33   Acts 10:39–41

    C.   He appeared to many after His resurrection.
        Matthew 28:9,17   Mark 16:9   Luke 24:15
        Luke 24:36,50   I Corinthians 15:5–8
        John 20:19,26   John 21:1   Acts 9:3–5

II.   **Then Jesus Christ ascended to God the Father and was exalted.**
        Mark 16:19   Philippians 2:9–11   Ephesians 1:19–22

III. **Jesus Christ is our Lord and King.**
        I Corinthians 8:6   Isaiah 9:6–7   I Corinthians 15:25
        Hebrews 10:12–13   Colossians 1:12–20
        Philippians 2:9–11

        Jesus Christ wants to be our Savior, our keeper, our physician, our Lord, and our King.

MEMORY VERSE

I Corinthians 15:25

Water Baptism

SCRIPTURE READINGS

Mark 16:15–20
Colossians 2:6–17

LESSON

I.   Who is to be baptized in water?
Mark 16:15–16

II.   Jesus commanded us to be baptized in water.
Matthew 28:19   Acts 2:38   Acts 10:47–48

III. What is the meaning of water baptism? What does it express?
Romans 6:3–4   Galatians 3:27   Colossians 2:12–13

IV.   How were people baptized in the Bible?
Mark 1:8–11   Acts 8:38–39

MEMORY VERSE

Galatians 3:27

Christian Living

SCRIPTURE READINGS

Colossians 3
Romans 6

LESSON

I.   **The Christian puts off the old life.**

A.   Sins are forbidden.
Romans 6:11–14   John 5:14

B.   Sins are to be forsaken.
Hebrews 12:1   Isaiah 55:7

C.   The Christian's desires are to be controlled.
I Peter 2:2,11

D.   The Christian's tongue is to be controlled.
James 1:26–27   James 3:2–13

E.   The Christian is to be a good example to others and is to love others.
John 13:34–35   Romans 14:13

II.   **The Christian enters a new life.**

A.   He has a new birth.
John 1:13   John 3:3,5

B.   He has a new heart.
Ezekiel 36:26

C.   He has a new realm to live in.
II Corinthians 5:17

D. He has new growth.
   II Peter 3:18

E. He has new food to eat.
   I Peter 2:2–3

F. He has new clothes.
   Isaiah 61:10

G. He has new light.
   Matthew 5:16

H. He has new life and character.
   Matthew 7:24–25

I. He has a new understanding.
   John 8:31–32

J. He has a new family.
   Ephesians 2:19–22

MEMORY VERSE

John 13:35

Prayer

SCRIPTURE READINGS

Luke 11:1–13
Luke 18:1–14
Matthew 6:5–18

LESSON

I.   **Why pray?**
     Matthew 7:7   Matthew 26:41

II. **When should we pray?**

     A.   Always.
          Luke 18:1   I Thessalonians 5:17   Ephesians 6:18

     B.   When in distress.
          Psalm 118:5   Psalm 18:6

     C.   When afflicted.
          James 5:13

III. **How should we pray?**

     A.   In Jesus' name.
          John 16:24   John 14:13–14

     B.   Believing and forgiving.
          Mark 11:24–26

     C.   In the Spirit.
          Ephesians 6:18

     D.   With the Holy Spirit's help.
          Romans 8:26–27

      E.   With confession of sin and with humility.
           II Chronicles 7:14

      F.   With your whole heart.
           Jeremiah 29:12–13

IV.   **Will your prayer be answered?**
      John 15:7   I John 3:22   I John 5:14–15

MEMORY VERSE

Hebrews 11:6

The Holy Spirit

SCRIPTURE READINGS

John 14
John 15:26–27
John 16:7–16
Acts 2

LESSON

I.   **Who is the Holy Spirit?**
     Matthew 28:19   John 15:26

II. **When and how did the Holy Spirit come?**
     Acts 2:1–21,37–41

III. **Why did the Holy Spirit come?**

    A.   To be an abiding Comforter.
          John 14:16–17 (KJV)

    B.   To teach us all things.
          John 14:26

    C.   To testify about Jesus.
          John 15:26

    D.   To convict.
          John 16:7–11

    E.   To guide us into all truth.
          John 16:13–15

    F.   To give us power to be Christ's witnesses.
          Acts 1:8

      G. To bear witness with our spirits.
          Romans 8:16

      H. To help us pray.
          Romans 8:26–27

IV.   Who may receive the Holy Spirit?
      Acts 2:37–39

MEMORY VERSES

John 16:8; John 16:13

Bible Study

SCRIPTURE READINGS

II Timothy 3:12—4:8
II Peter 1:19–21

LESSON

I. **The Bible is the inspired Word of God.**
II Peter 1:19–21   II Timothy 3:12–17

II. **Why should we study the Bible?**

A. God commands us to study His Word.
II Timothy 2:15 (KJV)

B. God delivers us through faith in His Word.
II Timothy 3:15   I Corinthians 15:1–4

C. God perfects us through His Word.
II Timothy 3:16–17

D. God gives us peace through His Word.
Psalm 119:165

E. God judges us by His Word.
John 12:48   Jeremiah 36

F. Neglect of the Word of God is destructive to our
spiritual life.
Hosea 4:6   Proverbs 29:18

G. By the Word of God we are able to attain real success
in living.
Joshua 1:8   Psalm 1

H. By the Word of God we are able to face the temptations of life.

Ephesians 6:11,17   Psalm 119:9–11

III. **How should we study the Bible?**

A. Do not neglect to read it.

B. Read it prayerfully, so that the Holy Spirit may reveal its meaning to you.

C. Read it systematically, not just a bit here and a bit there.

D. Use reference books to help you with the difficult passages. Use a good Bible dictionary, a Bible textbook, Halley's *Bible Handbook*, and a concordance (Young's *Analytical Concordance to the Bible*, Strong's *Exhaustive Concordance of the Bible*, or the *New American Standard Exhaustive Concordance of the Bible*).

E. Read it faithfully.

F. Memorize favorite passages and meditate upon them.

MEMORY VERSES

II Timothy 3:16–17

The Lord's Supper

LESSON

9

SCRIPTURE READINGS

I Corinthians 11:23–32 Luke 22:7–30
Matthew 26:17–30   John 13:1–30
Mark 14:12–26

LESSON

I. **The Lord's Supper was instituted by Jesus.**
  Matthew 26:26–28 Mark 14:22–24

II. **What is the purpose of the Lord's Supper?**
  I Corinthians 11:23–26 Luke 22:19–20

III. **Who may partake of the Lord's Supper?**
  I Corinthians 11:27–32

IV. **Examples of the Lord's Supper in the Scriptures.**
  Acts 2:42 Acts 20:7,11

MEMORY VERSE

I Corinthians 11:26

The Second Coming of Jesus Christ

SCRIPTURE READINGS

Matthew 24
I Thessalonians 4:13–18
I Thessalonians 5:1–11

LESSON

I. **His return was foretold.**

Acts 1:9–11   John 14:3   I Thessalonians 4:13–18

II. **The time of His return is unknown.**

Matthew 24:36–42   Luke 12:40

III. **What are the purposes of His coming?**

A. He is coming to be glorified **in His saints**, and to be admired **in all them that believe**.

II Thessalonians 1:7–12 (KJV)

This spiritual coming in His saints precedes His coming to the world. However, this spiritual coming is overlooked or not known by most of God's people.

B. He is coming to reward His saints for their works.

Matthew 16:27

C. He is coming to judge the ungodly.

Jude 14–15

IV. **What should our attitude be concerning His coming?**

    A. We should be ready.
       Matthew 24:44

    B. We should be waiting.
       I Corinthians 1:7–8

    C. We should be looking.
       Hebrews 9:28

    D. We should be working.
       Luke 19:13

V. **In the end time, a great revival is to come to prepare the saints for the Lord's coming, just as the rain prepares the fruit for harvest.**
James 5:7–11

Christ wants a Church that is pure and ready.
Ephesians 5:25–27

VI. **In the end time, the power and the miracles of the Bible will be restored to the Church.**
Acts 3:19–24

VII. **In the end time, great troubles will come to the earth.**
Daniel 12:1   Matthew 24:6–14,21–31

However, God's people will do great things for God.
Daniel 11:32   Daniel 12:9–10

VIII. **These end-time events will come upon the earth and men will be unaware that the day of the Lord is dawning.**
I Thessalonians 5:1–11

MEMORY VERSE

Luke 12:40

The Church

SCRIPTURE READINGS

Acts 2
Matthew 16:13–20

LESSON

The word "church" comes from the Greek word *ekklesia*, which means "that which is called out."

I. **The foundation of the Church.**

Matthew 16:16–18

Note carefully that the Bible speaks of only one true Church, and it was not divided into various sects or into denominations. We must pray for the coming oneness of the entire Body of Christ.

I Corinthians 3:1–4

II. **When was the Church established?**

Acts 2:1–4

III. **Who can become members of the Church, and how do they become members?**

Acts 2:41   Acts 2:47   Acts 5:14   Acts 11:24

IV. **How the members of the Church came to be called Christians.**

Acts 11:26

V. **Members of the Church should acknowledge and respect one another as brethren.**

Acts 9:17   Acts 21:20

VI. **Christ is the Head of the Church.**

Ephesians 1:22   Ephesians 5:23   Colossians 1:18

VII. The Church is the Body of Christ.

Ephesians 1:22–23   Colossians 1:24
I Corinthians 12:12–27

If we are members of the Body of Christ, God will set us in that Body where He wants us to serve Him.

I Corinthians 12:18

We must pray for God to set us in a local church that is built on the New Testament church pattern, where we can best worship and serve God. (Other lessons describe the local church and how it functions.)

VIII. The Church is the Bride of Christ.

II Corinthians 11:2   Revelation 19:7

MEMORY VERSE

Ephesians 5:30

Going On with God

SCRIPTURE READINGS

Hebrews 5:12—6:3
II Peter 3:17–18

LESSON

I. **Separate yourself from the old life.**

   II Corinthians 6:14—7:1   I Corinthians 8:1–13
   Ephesians 4:22–24

   Note especially the separation from idolatry.

II. **Always look to God, not to man, for all good comes from God.**

   James 1:17   John 3:27

III. **Worship only God, and make Him first in your heart.**

   Matthew 4:10   Luke 10:27

IV. **Remember that all power is given to Jesus Christ to back you up.**

   Matthew 11:27–28   Matthew 28:18–20
   Philippians 2:9–11   Romans 14:8–9

V. **Therefore, come to God in Jesus' name with confidence.**

   John 15:16   John 16:23–24

VI. **Go forward in Christ.**

   Isaiah 30:20–21   Luke 9:62   Philippians 3:14
   Philippians 4:13

VII. Always keep a right spirit before God.
Psalm 51:10,17   Isaiah 57:15

MEMORY VERSE

John 3:36

Faith

SCRIPTURE READING

Hebrews 11

LESSON

I.   **What is faith?**

It is believing God.
Hebrews 11:1

II. **We can please God only by our faith.**
Hebrews 11:6

III. **Our victory over the world and our success as believers is by our faith.**
I John 5:4   Galatians 5:6   Ephesians 6:16
Habakkuk 2:4

IV. **The greatest work we can do is to believe in Jesus Christ.**
John 6:28–29

V.   **Prayer with wavering and doubting is not answered. According to our faith we receive from God.**
James 1:5–7   Matthew 8:13   Matthew 9:29–30

VI. **All things are possible through faith.**
Matthew 17:20   Mark 9:23

VII. **How can we have more faith?**
Romans 10:17

MEMORY VERSE

Hebrews 11:1

Assembling Together

SCRIPTURE READINGS

Hebrews 10:23–27   I Corinthians 11:18–34
Acts 2:42,46–47   I Corinthians 14:23–40
Acts 20:7   I Corinthians 16:1–2

LESSON

I.   The assembling of the saints is not to be neglected, especially as the end time approaches.

Hebrews 10:23–27

II. Where should we assemble?

   A.   Where the Lord chooses.

Deuteronomy 12:5

   B.   Where the Lord places us.

I Corinthians 12:18

III. When should we gather together?

   A.   On the Sabbath.[1]

Acts 16:13   Acts 17:2

   B.   On the first day of the week.

Acts 20:7

Note that the early Church observed both the Sabbath and the first day of the week.

   C.   The book of Acts records other times when the early Church met together.

---

1. Refer to Lesson 33, item XXI.

1. From day to day, for sharing the Word, for fellowship, and for breaking bread.
   Acts 2:42,46–47

2. On special occasions.
   Acts 15:30–32

3. At the hour of prayer.
   Acts 3:1

4. In times of need.
   Acts 12:5,11–12

IV. **Why should we assemble together?**

A. To worship.
   Psalm 122:1–4

B. For the Lord's Supper and the ministry of the Word.
   Acts 2:42,46   Acts 20:7   I Corinthians 11:18–34

C. To bring tithes and offerings.
   I Corinthians 16:1–2

D. To edify and teach one another, and to minister in the Holy Spirit to one another.
   I Corinthians 14:23–40   Hebrews 10:24
   Colossians 3:16

E. To minister to one another because we need each other.
   I Corinthians 12:12–27

F. To observe the feasts of the Lord.
   Exodus 23:14–16   I Corinthians 5:7–8   Acts 20:16

   In this day, the Lord is restoring the spiritual observance of the feasts that He commanded His people Israel to keep as part of their worship.[2]

   ---
   2. Refer to Lesson 33, item XXII.

G. Because the Lord commands us to.
Hebrews 10:25

REVIEW QUESTIONS

1. When does your local church meet each week?

2. What purpose does each of these gatherings fill in your life? in the church?

3. How do you minister to the Lord? to each other?

MEMORY VERSE

Hebrews 10:25

Discerning the True from the False

SCRIPTURE READINGS

I John 2:18–29
I John 4:1–13

LESSON

I. **Do we need to know the true from the false?**
   I Kings 3:9   Isaiah 11:3   I Corinthians 2:14
   Hebrews 5:13–14

   A. Remember that Satan knows spiritual truths.
      Mark 1:24,34   Luke 4:41

   B. Satan sometimes uses Scriptures with great deception.
      II Corinthians 11:1–4,13–15

   C. When Satan does this, answer him with the Word of God.
      Matthew 4:1–11 — Deuteronomy 8:3

   D. Surely it is necessary for us to study the Word of God and to hide it in our hearts.
      Psalm 119:11

II. **How can we test the spirits to see if they are of God?**
    I John 4:1–3   I Corinthians 12:3

III. **How can we know if a teaching is true?**
     John 7:17

IV. **How can we know if a teacher or minister is sent by God?**

John 7:18

V. **Some examples of discernment.**

II Kings 6:12   Nehemiah 6:12   Luke 5:22
Acts 10:28,34–35

MEMORY VERSES

John 7:17–18

God's Financial Plan— the Tithe

SCRIPTURE READINGS

II Corinthians 8
II Corinthians 9
Hebrews 7:1–17

LESSON

I.   **Tithing before the Law—voluntary.**

   A.   Abraham paid tithes.
        Genesis 14:18–20

   B.   Jacob promised a tenth.
        Genesis 28:20–22

II. **Tithing under the Law of Moses—compulsory.**

   A.   The tithe belongs to God.
        Leviticus 27:30–32

   B.   Obedience to the law of tithing brings blessing on one's life.
        Malachi 3:10

   C.   How were the tithes that were collected used?
        Nehemiah 10:37–39   Numbers 18:25–31

III. **Tithing under grace—willingly.**

   A.   We pay our tithes to the priesthood after the order of Melchizedek.
        Hebrews 7:1–17

    B.   First we give ourselves to God; then we give our gifts and tithes.
        II Corinthians 8:5,11–12

    C.   We give cheerfully.
        II Corinthians 9:6–8

    D.   We give bountifully.
        Luke 6:38

    E.   When are we to give?
        I Corinthians 16:1–2

    F.   How are the tithes used?
        Matthew 10:7–10

    G.   How are the offerings used?
        II Corinthians 9:7–14

IV.   How are we to give gifts (not tithes) to the poor?
Matthew 6:1–4

MEMORY VERSE

II Corinthians 9:8

BREAD
FOR THE LITTLE
CHILDREN

Singing in the Spirit

SCRIPTURE READINGS

James 5:13
Ezra 3:10–11
Psalm 149
Acts 16:19–34
Ephesians 5:18–21
Colossians 3:12–17
I Corinthians 14:15,26

I Samuel 16:14–23
II Kings 3:11–27
I Chronicles 13, 15, and 16
I Chronicles 6:31–48
Nehemiah 12:27–30,45–47
Exodus 15:1–21

LESSON

I.   We are commanded to praise and sing by the Spirit of God.

Ephesians 5:18–21

II. We are commanded to do this with all our heart.

Colossians 3:12–17

III. When we sing in the Spirit, there is power in our services.

A. When David sang, the evil spirit left Saul.

I Samuel 16:14–23

B. Singing stimulated and encouraged the prophet in his ministry.

II Kings 3:11–27

C. As the apostles sang, God opened the prison doors.

Acts 16:19–34

    D.   Singing was a strong weapon of God to bring victory in battle.

        II Chronicles 20

    E.   David appointed singers to sing and worship continually before the presence of the Lord.

        I Chronicles 6:31–48   I Chronicles 13, 15, and 16

        This Tabernacle of David is being restored today.

        Acts 15:13–19

    F.   Psalms come to us to praise God for His deliverance.

        Exodus 15:1–21

IV.   When we sing in the Spirit, we are moving in prophecy.

    A.   Distinguish singing in the Spirit from natural singing.

        I Corinthians 14:15,26

    B.   Distinguish worship and singing in the Spirit from psalms, hymns, and spiritual songs.

        Colossians 3:12–17

    C.   There are those who prophesy with harps and other musical instruments.

        I Chronicles 25:1–7

        This prophetic ministry of music was restored in the days of Ezra and Nehemiah.

        Nehemiah 12:27–30,45–47   Ezra 3:10–11

    D.   There is a difference between singing the Word of the Lord and singing the word of man.

REVIEW QUESTIONS

1.   What is the difference between singing in the Spirit and singing out of hymn books?

2.   What miraculous things happened when men in the Bible were anointed to sing? Name as many incidents as you can from the lesson.

3.   Do you think that singing psalms in the Spirit is a manifestation of the gift of prophecy?

4.   Why is singing in the Spirit important to the services?

Our Worship

SCRIPTURE READINGS

Psalm 95
John 4:19–24
Colossians 3:15–16
Malachi 3:16—4:2

LESSON

I.   **We should sing unto the Lord.**
     Psalm 95:1

II. **We should praise the Lord and give Him thanksgiving.**
     Psalm 95:2–5   Colossians 3:15–16

III. **We should worship the Lord.**
     Psalm 95:6–7a

   A. What is worship? In the Hebrew, "worship" means
       "to bow yourself down" in adoring contemplation
       of God. Worship is more than reading the Bible and
       meditating on it. Worship is more than listening to a
       sermon. Worship is more than most singing and
       praying. Prayer is concerned with our needs; praise
       is concerned with our blessings; worship is con-
       cerned with loving and adoring God Himself.

   B. Here are some scriptural examples of worship.
       Exodus 33:10   Exodus 34:5–8   Joshua 5:13–14
       II Chronicles 7:3

   C. What did Jesus teach us about worship?
       John 4:19–24

       1. We should worship God only.
           Matthew 4:10

2.   The Father seeks true worshipers.
     John 4:23

     The book of Revelation speaks fourteen times
     of the worship which will fill all eternity.[1]

3.   The place of worship is not important.
     John 4:19–21

4.   We must worship in spirit and in truth.
     John 4:24

D.   True worship satisfies God.
     John 4:23

     1.   The worshiper also receives spiritual
          satisfaction.
          Psalm 16:11

     2.   The worshiper is humbled and strengthened.

IV. **We should reverence and fear the Lord.**
     Psalm 95:7b–11   Malachi 3:16—4:2

     A.   The fear of the Lord is part of our worship.
          Psalm 2:11   Psalm 89:7

     B.   The fear of the Lord is necessary.
          Hebrews 12:28 (KJV)   II Corinthians 7:1
          Exodus 20:20

     C.   Note what the reverence and fear of the Lord bring to
          you.

          1.   The fear of the Lord is the beginning of wisdom.
               Proverbs 9:10

---

1.   Refer to Appendix A.

2. The fear of the Lord gives pleasure to God.
   Psalm 147:11

3. The fear of the Lord brings mercy and pity from God.
   Psalm 103:11,13,17

4. The fear of the Lord brings blessing.
   Psalm 112:1   Psalm 115:13

5. The fear of the Lord brings the heart's desires.
   Psalm 145:19

6. The fear of the Lord brings long life.
   Proverbs 10:27

7. The fear of the Lord brings purity.
   Proverbs 16:6

8. The fear of the Lord brings satisfaction.
   Proverbs 19:23

9. The fear of the Lord gives confidence.
   Proverbs 14:26

10. The fear of the Lord eliminates other fears.
    Isaiah 8:12–13

Understanding

Who shall understand spiritual things?
How shall we know the truth?

SCRIPTURE READINGS

John 8:31–32,43–47   II Corinthians 4:4
Romans 1:18–32   John 7:15–18
II Corinthians 3:14–15   Matthew 11:25–26

INTRODUCTION

We have a faculty by which we know true doctrine when we hear it. That faculty is not a mental power; it is an ability of our spirit which is God-given to those who will do the will of God.

LESSON

I. How does fuller revelation and understanding come to us?

    A. By pressing on to know the Lord.
       Hosea 6:3

    B. By continuing in His Word—then we know the truth.
       John 8:31–32,43–47

II. The capacity to see the truth is God-given and is retained as we will to do His will. God opens and closes eyes.

    A. "It is given to you to know."
       Matthew 13:11–12

    B.   Israel was blinded because of rebellion.

        Isaiah 6:9–12   Matthew 13:10–17 (note verse 14)
        Ezekiel 12:2

    C.   Sinning against the truth brings a darkened heart and a reprobate (depraved) mind.

        Romans 1:18–32

    D.   Unbelief puts a veil over the heart.

        II Corinthians 3:14–15   Romans 11:25–26

    E.   Satan blinds the minds of those who do not believe.

        II Corinthians 4:4

    F.   Sin darkens the understanding.

        Ephesians 4:18

III. The most precious thing you have is your spiritual sight.

    A.   Take heed how you hear the truth.

        Mark 4:23–25

    B.   The pure in heart shall see God.

        Matthew 5:8

    C.   Some are ever learning, yet never able to come to the knowledge of the truth. They have no capacity to know the truth.

        II Timothy 3:7

IV. Our spiritual understanding depends upon our having a willing and obedient heart, not upon our natural wisdom.

    A.   If you will to do His will, you shall know.

        John 7:15–18

B. To him who has shall more be given.
    Matthew 13:12

C. An anointing is necessary.
    Revelation 3:18

The Family

SCRIPTURE READINGS

Ephesians 5:22—6:4
Titus 2:1–8
Colossians 3:18–21
I Peter 3:1–12

LESSON

I. **The family should be a spiritual unit.**
    Matthew 19:3–6

    A. Marriage was divinely instituted to create a unit.
        Genesis 2:18–25

    B. God instructed the first family.
        Genesis 1:26–28

        1. Be fruitful and multiply.

        2. Fill the earth.

        3. Subdue the earth and rule over it.
            A godly family is a powerful thing.

    C. The "spirit" of the marriage is important.
        Malachi 2:13–16

    D. Husbands and wives are interdependent.
        I Corinthians 11:11–12

II. **The head of the family is the father.**
    I Corinthians 11:3   Genesis 3:16   Ephesians 5:23

III. Responsibilities of parents.

A. To love.

Ephesians 5:25,28   Psalm 103:13   Titus 2:3–4

B. To teach.

Deuteronomy 6:6–9   Deuteronomy 11:18–21
Deuteronomy 4:9–10

C. To discipline.

Proverbs 13:24   Proverbs 29:15,17   Proverbs 19:18
Proverbs 22:15

D. To train.

Proverbs 22:6

IV. Responsibilities of husbands and fathers.

A. To love with a self-sacrificing love.
Ephesians 5:25,28,33

B. To nourish and cherish the family.
Ephesians 5:28–30

C. To love without bitterness or resentment.
Colossians 3:19

D. To treat their wives with understanding, respect, and honor.
I Peter 3:7

E. To bear responsibility.
Numbers 30, especially verses 13–15

F. To teach and to lead.
Ephesians 6:4

G. Fathers should not provoke their children to anger.
Colossians 3:21

V. **Responsibilities of wives and mothers.**

A. To be submissive to their husbands.
    Ephesians 5:22–24   Colossians 3:18   I Peter 3:1–2

    This submission is not to be a suppression of the wife.

B. To respect their husbands.
    Ephesians 5:33   I Peter 3:6

C. To love the family, to keep the home, to be self-controlled.
    Titus 2:3–5

D. To have the inner quality of a gentle and peaceful spirit.
    I Peter 3:1–6

E. A picture of an excellent wife.
    Proverbs 31:10–31

VI. **Responsibilities of children.**

A. To honor their parents.
    Exodus 20:12   Ephesians 6:1–3

    This commandment has the promise of long life.

B. To be obedient.
    Colossians 3:20   Ephesians 6:1

C. To accept discipline.
    Proverbs 3:11–12   Proverbs 13:1

VII. **The answer for every family problem.**
    Matthew 6:33

VIII. Scriptural covenants and promises for your family and relatives.

Read Genesis 12:1–3, Genesis 17:1–7, and
Genesis 26:23–24 with Galatians 3:25–29.

Read Exodus 12:1–27 with I Corinthians 5:6–11.

Acts 16:19–34   Isaiah 49:25   Acts 2:38–39
Psalm 103:17–18   Jeremiah 32:39

Isaiah 44:3   Isaiah 54:13

Fruitfulness

SCRIPTURE READINGS

Psalm 1:2–3
James 5:7–8
Isaiah 55:10–13
John 15

LESSON

I. **What is meant by "fruit"?**

    A. Fruit of the Spirit.
        Galatians 5:22–23

    B. Fruit of prayer and worship.
        Isaiah 56:4–8   Hebrews 13:15

    C. Fruit of works (living works).
        Colossians 1:9–11

    D. Fruit of giving.
        Philippians 4:15–19   Romans 15:25–29

    E. Fruit of souls.
        John 4:35–39   Isaiah 49:19–25   Isaiah 66:18–21

        1. Bring forth fruit (sons) to Christ.
            Romans 7:4

        2. A promise to the barren.
            Isaiah 54

  F. Fruit of ministries.
   Colossians 1:24–29

 II. **God preserves the fruitful.**
  Deuteronomy 20:19–20

  Fruit trees were preserved in war.

 III. **God judges those who do not bear fruit in season.**
  Luke 13:6–9 Hebrews 6:7–9 Isaiah 5:1–6

 IV. **What is necessary for fruitfulness?**

  A. Water (the Word).
   Psalm 1:2–3 Isaiah 55:10–13

  B. Cultivated soil (receptivity).
   Matthew 13:23

  C. Death.
   John 12:24

  D. Pruning.
   John 15:2

  E. Abiding in the vine.
   John 15:5

Healing and Health

SCRIPTURE READINGS

Isaiah 53:3–5
I John 3:8
Mark 16:17–18
I Peter 2:24

Exodus 15:26
Matthew 8:16–17
Psalm 103:2–3
Mark 11:24

INTRODUCTION

Sickness and sin came to mankind through the fall in the
Garden of Eden. There is no sin, disease, death, sorrow, or
curse mentioned in the first two chapters of Genesis or in the
last two chapters of Revelation. Genesis 3 tells of the fall into
sin and the judgment that came upon the world, with disease,
death, thorns, sorrow, and pain. However, God then promised a
Redeemer who would remove the curse from us (Genesis 3:15).

LESSON

I. **The Lord Jesus Christ bore our sins and sicknesses so
    that we might be forgiven and healed.**

    Isaiah 53:3–5   Matthew 8:16–17   I John 3:8

    A. Jesus associated sin with sickness.

        Mark 2:1–12

    B. It has been said that nine-tenths of Jesus' ministry
        was healing the sick. Do you think this is true?

II. **Some examples of healing the sick in the Scriptures.**

    A. Before Christ.

        Exodus 15:26   Psalm 105:37 (KJV)
        II Chronicles 16:12–13   II Kings 20:1–11

B.   During Christ's time.

Jesus healed, even though there were many physicians in His day (Mark 5:26). Twenty-four cases of healing are recorded by Luke, the beloved physician.[1] Jesus healed people in many places, at many times, using many different methods.

1.   When Jesus healed there was instant recovery in most cases. He healed some and they began to get better from that very hour (John 4:52–53). He healed others and the results were apparent soon afterward (Luke 17:14).

2.   Jesus healed those far away (16 miles away, John 4:46–54) and in the midst of crowded multitudes (Mark 1:32–34). He healed by a touch, by others touching Him, by taking them by the hand, by giving a command, and by speaking a Word.

3.   Jesus healed all manner of diseases (Matthew 4:23–24), including lunacy, epilepsy, leprosy, palsy, fever, paralysis, blindness, lameness, deafness, and withered limbs. He restored an ear severed by a sword.

4.   He healed chronic cases also: the woman who had a hemorrhage for 12 years (Luke 8:43–48); the cripple bowed over for 18 years (Luke 13:11–13); the lame man beside the pool of Bethesda, crippled for 38 years (John 5:5–9).

5.   Jesus transmitted the power to heal to others: to the twelve disciples (Matthew 10:1,8); to the 70 disciples (Luke 10:1–9); and to believers in general who claim the power (Mark 16:17–18). It

---

1.   Refer to Appendix B.

was transmitted to Peter's shadow (Acts 5:15) and to Paul's handkerchiefs (Acts 19:12).

    C.   In the early Church.

        1.   Over 20 years after Christ, Paul had power to heal.

            Acts 19:12   Acts 28:7–9

        2.   Twenty-four years after Christ, ordinary believers had the gifts of healing.

            I Corinthians 12:9   Galatians 3:5

        3.   Twenty-seven years after Christ, James gave directions for healing the sick.

            James 5:13–16

        4.   Over a century after Christ, Irenaeus wrote, *"Others still, heal the sick by laying their hands upon them, and they are made whole."*[2]

        5.   There are many other references to healing in the early Church writings, too numerous to include.

    D.   In modern times we also have the testimony of many miracles of healing in answer to prayer.

III.   Scriptural promises to claim for healing.
Mark 16:17–18   Psalm 103:2–3   I Peter 2:24
Mark 11:24   Jeremiah 32:27   Jeremiah 33:3

IV.   Suggestions for the sick who want to be healed.
I John 3:20–23   I John 5:14–15

    A.   Search your heart and repent of sin.

    B.   Know the Scriptures that promise your healing.

---

   2. IRENAEUS, *Against Heresies*, bk. 2, chap. 32, par. 4.

C.   Ask God for faith to believe His promises.

D.   If necessary, seek help from those who have faith.

V.   **Scriptural ways of receiving healing.**

The first four ways are given in James 5:13–16.

A.   By the afflicted person praying.
     James 5:13   Psalm 119:67,71

B.   Through the sick believer calling the elders to anoint him with oil and pray for him.
     James 5:14–15

C.   Through the church's humility and confession, and by praying one for another.
     James 5:16

D.   Through fervent intercession.
     James 5:16

E.   Through the laying on of hands or a touch.
     Mark 16:15–20   Matthew 8:2–4,14–15
     Luke 22:50–51   Acts 28:8

F.   Through a spoken word.
     John 4:46–54   Matthew 8:5–13   Luke 13:10–17
     Luke 18:35–43

G.   Through the person who is sick touching the one with an anointing to heal.
     Luke 8:43–48   Mark 6:56

H.   Through prayer in Jesus' name.
     Acts 3:6   Acts 9:33–35   Acts 16:16–18

I.   Through the Holy Spirit directing an individual by revelation to impart healing to the one who is sick.
     Acts 9:11–18   Acts 14:8–10

J. Through the use of unusual means.
    Mark 7:31–37   Mark 8:22–26   John 9:1–7
    Acts 5:15–16   Acts 19:11–12   Acts 20:9–10

K. Through action taken by the sick one to show faith.
    John 5:1–9   Matthew 9:1–7   Luke 17:11–19

L. Through the faith of the one who is sick.
    Matthew 9:27–31

M. Through hearing the Word of God.

    He sent His word and healed them.... Psalm 107:20.

Deliverance I

SCRIPTURE READINGS

Isaiah 42:6–10
John 8:31–48

LESSON

I. **What is deliverance?**

Deliverance is the breaking of **spiritual bondage** in your life. This bondage may be caused by:

A. People.

B. Circumstances.

C. Demons.

D. Physical infirmities.

E. Inner self and inner desires.

F. Even good things taken to excess.

II. **How is deliverance ministered?**

A major hurdle to ministering deliverance is accurately detecting and defining the need. When spiritual bondage exists in your life, you rarely see it yourself. Others also tend to evaluate your need from their own point of view rather than by a revelation of the Holy Spirit. The story of Job is an illustration of this.

Job 38:1–2

A. As you wait on the Lord,[1] your own need can be revealed by the Spirit; then seek help.

---

1. Refer to Lesson 45.

B. Revelation may also come through others by discernment, by the Word of knowledge, or by the Word of wisdom.

C. Means of deliverance.

1. Deliver yourself.

2. "You shall know the truth, and the truth shall make you free."
   John 8:32

3. Deliverance at the Communion table.
   I Corinthians 11:24–32

4. Deliverance through others.
   James 5:14–20

5. Deliverance through angels and supernatural phenomena.

   a. Lot and his family by angels.
      Genesis 19:1–29

   b. The three Hebrews from the fiery furnace.
      Daniel 3

   c. Daniel from the lion's den.
      Daniel 6

   d. The apostles from prison.
      Acts 5:12–42

   e. Peter from prison by an angel.
      Acts 12:1–19

   f. Paul and Silas by an earthquake at Philippi.
      Acts 16:16–40

III. **How should we receive deliverance?**

The one who is seeking deliverance must be receptive. God's servants can minister only where their ministry is accepted. God's true instrument must be received.

Matthew 10:40   Proverbs 1:7   John 12:47–48

It is important to remember that deliverance is wrought through lowly vessels, as was true of Samson, Gideon, Jonah, and many other biblical characters.

I Corinthians 1:26–29

Keep your eyes on the Lord, never on the person who is used as the instrument of deliverance.

IV. **A great example of a right spirit in giving and receiving ministry.**

I Thessalonians 2

V. **Do not associate the need for a deliverance with condemnation and guilt.**

A. Remember that deliverance comes for the glory of God.

John 9:1–7

B. Remember that deliverance is promised for the godly.

II Peter 2:9

C. Remember that trials are common to man, and deliverance is provided.

No temptation (literally "trial," or "proving," or "attempt") *has overtaken you but such as is common to man; and God is faithful, who will not allow you to be tempted beyond what you are able, but with the temptation will provide the way of escape also* (literally "exit, a way out"), *that you may be able to endure it.* I Corinthians 10:13.

Deliverance II

SCRIPTURE READINGS

Daniel 7
Daniel 11:32–35
Daniel 12:10

LESSON

I.   **What God is doing—and what Satan is doing.**
     Daniel 12:10   Daniel 11:32–35

   A.   God is purifying and trying the saints.

   B.   Satan is inciting the wicked to do wickedly.

II. **Satan and his power.**

   A.   Scriptural names for Satan.

   Apollyon and Abaddon, the accuser of the brethren, the adversary, Belial, Beelzebub, the Devil, the god of this world (or age), the prince of the power of the air, the ruler (prince, KJV) of this world, the serpent, the wicked one.[1]

   B.   Satan's power.

   1.   Blinds the minds of unbelievers.
        II Corinthians 4:3–4

   2.   Comes with "all power and signs and lying wonders."
        II Thessalonians 2:9

---

   1.   Refer to Appendix C.

3. We do not wrestle against flesh and blood.
Ephesians 6:12 (KJV)

4. Jesus called him "the ruler of this world" three times.
John 12:31   John 14:30   John 16:11

5. Paul called him "the god of this age" and "the prince of the power of the air."
II Corinthians 4:3–4   Ephesians 2:2

C. Satan's demon spirits.

1. Satan is the prince of the power of the air.
Ephesians 2:2

2. Satan is king over demon powers.
Revelation 9:11

3. We wrestle against spiritual forces of wickedness in the heavenly places.
Ephesians 6:12

4. Demons are extremely numerous. They swarm the atmosphere, seeking embodiment in men and beasts. Mark 5:8–9 describes a man who was possessed by a legion of demons. (A legion is 3,000 to 6,000.)

a. Demon oppression—especially against saints (physically and spiritually).
Acts 10:38   Ephesians 6:12   I Peter 5:8–9

b. Demon possession.
Matthew 8:28   Mark 9:17–22   Luke 4:33

D. Different natures and personalities of demonic spirits.

Familiar spirit, spirit of jealousy, evil spirit, sorrowful spirit, lying spirit, haughty spirit, perverse spirit, spirit of deep sleep, spirit of heaviness, spirit of harlotry, unclean spirit, wicked spirit, seducing spirit, mute spirit, deaf spirit, foul spirit, spirit of infirmity, spirit of bondage, spirit of slumber, spirit of antichrist, spirit of error, spirit of demons, spirit of criticism, rebellious spirit, spirit of fear, spirit of strife and division.[2]

III. **Christ has won the victory over sin and Satan, and He gives us authority over these demonic and satanic powers.**

Matthew 28:16–20   Mark 13:34 (KJV)   Luke 10:17–19

On His cross, Christ canceled Satan's claims on earth and humanity.

IV. **We are empowered to enforce Christ's victory over all demons and disease through our anointing to use the name of Jesus.**

John 12:31   John 16:7–14   Daniel 7:13–18
Daniel 7:21–22   Daniel 7:25–27   Matthew 16:19

We must apply Christ's victory, or it remains an unused provision in our lives.

V. **When your life is emptied of demonic oppression, let Christ fill your life.**

A spiritual vacuum is dangerous.

Matthew 12:43–45   James 4:7

2. Refer to Appendix D.

Growth and Development

SCRIPTURE READINGS

John 16:12–15
Hebrews 5:11—6:3
I John 2:14
Hebrews 3:12–14

Matthew 24:44–51
I Peter 2:1–3
Hebrews 2:1–4
Colossians 1:28–29

LESSON

I. **Deeper understanding of the Scriptures comes with spiritual growth.**

One of the most important things for spiritually young believers to understand is that they cannot always comprehend or understand all the Scriptures. Fuller revelation and knowledge are often withheld until they are able to receive it.

John 16:12–15   John 13:7   John 16:25–27

Occasionally, the young believer hears or reads things that almost overwhelm him. When this happens, he must not be disturbed, but must do as Peter instructs.

II Peter 3:14–18.

One of the outstanding aspects of Jesus' ministry was the way that He taught, being careful to give the people only what they could receive. That is why He taught by parables.

Matthew 13:10–17

II. **There is a blessing for the steward who ministers meat in due season as the believers are able to receive it.**
Matthew 24:44–51

The book of Hebrews also speaks about withholding the meat of the Word until the people are able to receive it.
Hebrews 5:11–6:3.

Note the "dullness of hearing" (verse 11), which is the great hindrance to spiritual growth.

III. **Babes should desire undiluted milk.**
I Peter 2:1–3

The pure Word is one of the best and greatest means of spiritual growth. When the Word of God abides in you, you will grow out of the "baby" stage and soon enter into the "young man" stage.
I John 2:14

IV. **The spiritual elements of a believer grow.**

Note that your faith and love can grow.
II Thessalonians 1:3   I Thessalonians 3:12–13
I Thessalonians 4:9–12

V. **Regularity in church attendance is helpful for growth and development, especially in times of testing.**
Hebrews 10:22–25

VI. **There is nothing more dangerous than neglect.**
Hebrews 2:1–4

Remember that when people lose out with God, there is little feeling or pain involved. The heart is hardened and, like Samson, they do not know that the Lord has departed from them (Judges 16:20). The time to help people is while they are in the church, before their hearts become hardened.
Hebrews 3:12–14

It is easier to prevent a problem than to fix it.

VII. **The divinely appointed ministries are a very important means of spiritual growth and development. These are the "spiritual nurses" who will feed you and minister to you.**

Ephesians 4:11–16   Galatians 6:1–2   James 5:19–20

The picture here is one of older children helping the younger children in the family.

VIII. **It should be settled in our minds that only mature perfection in Christ Jesus will satisfy the Father in heaven.**

Colossians 1:28–29   James 1:4   I Corinthians 13:11
Matthew 5:48

We are constantly being tested in our faith and exercised in righteousness, that we might grow.

IX. **A secret of growth.**

We do not grow by our effort, but by exposing ourselves to the moving of the Lord and to His Word. The Lord works the change and development in us.

II Corinthians 3:18

X. **A practical warning.**

Avoid rash promises and vows to the Lord, because you can produce very little by yourself. Rather, look to the Lord when He deals with your heart about a matter and purpose in your heart to be obedient, looking for grace from God to accomplish it.

Personal Ministry

SCRIPTURE READINGS

Acts 9:10–19
Matthew 10:1–8
James 5:14–16
I Timothy 4:14
Acts 22:6–21
Mark 6:7–13

Matthew 28:18–20
I Timothy 1:18–19
Luke 10:1–20
Isaiah 58:6–12
Acts 19:1–7
II Timothy 1:6–7

LESSON

I.   **What is personal ministry?**

Personal ministry is the experiencing or receiving of a scriptural experience of blessing through the spiritual help of one or more ministries in the Body of Christ. An example is found in Acts 9:10–19 and also in Acts 22:6–21. These passages describe how Ananias ministered to Saul of Tarsus. Saul, later called Paul, received assurance of salvation, healing of his blindness, water baptism, the baptism of the Holy Spirit, and a personal prophecy of experiences to come.

Thus, personal ministry is the giving of a scriptural experience or gift to an individual believer. For example, if a believer is sick and the elders anoint him with oil and pray for him and he is healed (James 5:14), he has received personal ministry which has brought him an experience of healing.

II. **Does the Lord give His servants ministry for them to give to others?**

Yes; freely you receive, freely you give.

Matthew 10:1,7–8   Mark 6:7,12–13   Luke 9:1–2
Luke 10:1–9,17–20   Ephesians 3:7   Colossians 1:28–29

III. **What experiences or gifts may I receive through other believers ministering to me?**

A. Deliverance and forgiveness of sin.
John 20:21–23   Matthew 16:19
Matthew 18:18–20   Isaiah 58:6–12

B. Ordinances of the Church.

1. Water baptism.
Matthew 28:18–20   Mark 16:15–16

2. The Lord's Supper.
I Corinthians 11:23–26

3. Foot washing.
John 13:3–17

C. Healing and deliverance from demonic oppression.
Mark 16:17–18   James 5:14–16

D. The baptism of the Holy Spirit.
Acts 8:14–17   Acts 19:1–7

E. Gifts of the Holy Spirit.
I Timothy 4:14   II Timothy 1:6–7

F. Personal directive prophecy.
I Timothy 1:18–19   I Timothy 4:14

The laying on of hands may be the means of imparting most of the experiences listed above. It is also the means of setting apart and ordaining ministries, such as the elders of the local church, deacons, apostles, prophets, pastors, and others.

I Timothy 5:17–22   Acts 6:5–6   Acts 13:1–4

IV.   Can several of these experiences and gifts be given to a believer at one time?

Yes.

Acts 9:17–19   Acts 19:6   Acts 10:43–48

V.   What caution should be given to those seeking personal ministry?

The believer should seek and accept ministry only from those ministries who are endowed by the Holy Spirit and commissioned by the Lord Jesus Christ to impart that ministry. Ordination or commission by a religious organization does not necessarily mean that a person has anything to impart. A ministry is God-given, not man-given. Much confusion and disappointment have resulted from "empty" hands being laid on seekers. Certainly a ministry cannot impart what he does not have.

The believer should seek instruction and guidance from the ministries who are able to lead him by the wisdom of God.

I Timothy 4:1–3,6   II Timothy 4:3–5   II Peter 2:1–3
Acts 19:24–30

The Gifts of the Holy Spirit

SCRIPTURE READINGS

I Corinthians 12
I Corinthians 14
Ephesians 1:15–23
John 14:10–17

LESSON

I.   **What is a gift of the Holy Spirit?**

A gift is the Holy Spirit's endowment of power, or revelation, or utterance. It is a divine enablement whereby a believer may speak or minister by the Holy Spirit with power or wisdom beyond his own abilities.

II. **What are the purposes and values of the gifts of the Spirit?**

A. The gifts are given to continue Christ's ministry to the world.

John 14:10–17   Ephesians 1:15–23

B. The gifts are given to build up the members of the Body of Christ.

I Corinthians 14:12,26   I Corinthians 12:7

C. The gifts are given to meet the spiritual and physical needs of every believer in the Body of Christ, whether that be for guidance, reproof, miraculous deliverance, healing, encouragement, comfort, or any other need.

I Corinthians 14:23–26,31   I Corinthians 14:1

III. What are the different gifts of the Holy Spirit?
I Corinthians 12:8–11

A. The Word of wisdom—a supernatural gift by the Holy Spirit of revelation and wisdom from God. It brings a Word of God's wisdom concerning His plans and purposes for an individual or a group.

B. The Word of knowledge—a supernatural gift by the Holy Spirit of revelation or knowledge. It brings a Word of God's knowledge of any fact.

C. Faith—a supernatural endowment of faith, given by the Holy Spirit.

D. Gifts of healings—supernatural gifts by the Holy Spirit to divinely heal the sick.

E. Working (or effecting) of miracles—a supernatural endowment by the Holy Spirit of power to perform miracles.

F. Prophecy—a supernatural gift to give utterances by the Holy Spirit in a language known to the speaker and hearers.

G. Discerning (or distinguishing) of spirits—a supernatural endowment by the Holy Spirit to detect the source of a spiritual manifestation, whether it is from God, from Satan, from demons, or from a human spirit.

H. Various kinds of tongues—a supernatural gift by the Holy Spirit to speak languages that the speaker has never learned.

I. Interpretation of tongues—a supernatural gift by the Holy Spirit to interpret languages that the speaker has never learned.

IV.   **Should we desire these gifts of the Holy Spirit?**

I Corinthians 12:31   I Corinthians 14:1–2

V.   **Can we receive some of these gifts of the Holy Spirit?**

I Corinthians 12:11   Romans 12:6

VI.   **How are the gifts of the Holy Spirit given?**

I Timothy 4:14   Romans 1:11   II Timothy 1:6
I Corinthians 12:11

The Local Church

SCRIPTURE READINGS

Acts 20:17–38
Matthew 18:15–20
Acts 13:1–4
Acts 6:1–6
I Corinthians 5

I Timothy 3:1–13
Acts 2:38–47
I Peter 5:1–4
Titus 1:5–9

LESSON

I. **Is the Church, the Body of Christ, a divine or a human institution?**

Is it built by man's promotion and organization, or is it built by God?

Matthew 16:15–20   Ephesians 2:20–22

II. **What is a local church?**

It is the congregation of believers in a certain locality.

I Corinthians 1:2   Galatians 1:2   II Corinthians 1:1
Philippians 1:1   I Thessalonians 1:1
II Thessalonians 1:1

III. **How are members received into the local church?**

Acts 2:38–41,47

A. In the book of Acts, believers were baptized in water and added to the church. Church membership has been abused and in most cases has become just a form. It should be approached spiritually, with recognition, both on the part of the new member and on the part of the elders and other members of the local body, that the Holy Spirit has set the new member in that church. The new member should also agree to submit to the authority of the elders and to the discipline of the church.

B. Adding members to the church is a spiritual work of the Holy Spirit. We should be faithful to keep simple records (name, address, and phone number) for the purpose of future ministry to them.

C. New members should publicly declare their personal faith in Jesus Christ, as well as the fact that they were led to the local church by the Holy Spirit and have been set in or added to that church. This should be confirmed by the elders and believers of the church. A biblical example in which a brother had difficulty establishing that he was a member of the church is found in Acts 9:26–28.

IV. **What is discipline in the local church?**

Matthew 18:15–20
I Corinthians 5 with II Corinthians 2:6–8

V. **What are the duties of the elders (or overseers) of the local church?**

I Peter 5:1–4   Acts 20:17,28,35,38

Local believers who are ordained by the Holy Spirit to serve the local church as overseers are spiritual ministries over the spiritual affairs of the church.

VI. **How are the elders ordained in the local church?**

In the early Church, elders were always appointed and ordained by the foundational ministries (apostles and prophets) and the other elders (if any).

Acts 14:23   Titus 1:5   Acts 20:28

Fasting and prayer are usually connected with the ordaining of elders.

Acts 13:2–3   Acts 14:23

The Holy Spirit may indicate that one of the members of the local church be made an elder. (Often the person is already manifesting a measure of the ministry.) The other ministries will encourage the individual to fast and pray about it and may also bring the matter before the

Body to fast and pray. If, after a period of testing, no reason for disqualification is found, the other elders, pastors, apostles, and prophets will lay hands on the person and ordain the individual as an elder (I Timothy 3:1–7; Titus 1:6–9). We can expect prophetic confirmation to the commission.

I Timothy 1:18–19

Hands should not be laid upon any man suddenly.

I Timothy 5:22 (Note from the context that this passage speaks of ordaining elders.)

VII. What are the qualifications of elders or bishops (overseers)?

I Timothy 3:1–7   Titus 1:5–9

Bishops or overseers are elders. The terms are used interchangeably.

Acts 20:17,28   Titus 1:5,7

VIII. What are the obligations of a congregation to its elders?

I Timothy 5:1,17–22   Hebrews 13:7,17

IX. What is the work of deacons and deaconesses in the local church?

Acts 6:1–3

They are believers who serve by the Holy Spirit in the temporal and spiritual affairs and business of the church.

X. What are the qualifications of deacons?

I Timothy 3:8–13   Acts 6:1–6

XI. **How are the deacons ordained in the local church?**
Acts 6:1–6

Deacons are sought out by the people and proved as to their ministry and qualifications (I Timothy 3:10). Then they are ordained by the laying on of hands by the foundational ministries and elders.
Acts 6:5–6

XII. **How are ministries to be sent forth?**

A. They are ordained and sent by the local church.
Acts 13:1–4

B. They are sent with communication recommending them to the other local churches.
Acts 14:26   I Corinthians 16:3
II Corinthians 3:1   Romans 16:1

C. Note that Paul and Barnabas returned to the local church and gave a full account to them of what had happened in their ministry.
Acts 14:26–28

XIII. **How are disputes between churches and questions over doctrines settled?**
Acts 15

A. Disputes are settled by a meeting of the foundational ministries and elders of the churches, with the Holy Spirit giving the answers. In the account given in Acts 15:7–19,32, the apostles and prophets mainly did the speaking.

B.   In the New Testament, the apostles determined the doctrine that was to be taught.

Acts 2:42   Acts 16:4–5   I Corinthians 4:17
I Corinthians 11:1–2   II Timothy 2:1–2
Philippians 4:9

This does not mean that an apostle is infallible.

Galatians 2:11–14

CONCLUSION

The curse of sectarianism would be removed from the churches forever if every church were built on this New Testament pattern.

Sectarianism

SCRIPTURE READINGS

John 17	Acts 2:41–47
I Corinthians 3	Acts 5:11–16
Romans 8:5–14	Ephesians 4:16
Galatians 5:19–21	Philippians 1:27—2:4

I Corinthians 12 (note verses 12,27)
Genesis 11:1–9 with Revelation 17 and 18

LESSON

I.   The Church is not a building; the Church is a body of redeemed people.

I Corinthians 12:27

II.   The Church is not a denomination or an organization or a sect.

Sectarian names are just tags which men have tacked onto the Body of Christ. These names are given because of men's pride and self-will and their desire to retain their identity. They seek to organize and make a name for themselves. This is the source of much religious confusion in the world today.

III.   All sectarianism is carnal.

I Corinthians 1:12   I Corinthians 3:3–4

The early Church had only four names of division: Paul, Apollos, Cephas, and Christ. The Church today has countless names of division. "Are you not fleshly (carnal), and walking like mere men?"

I Corinthians 3:3

There is no Scripture authorizing the present divisions and organizations of Christianity.

IV. **This carnality of sectarianism is sin and death to the Church.**

Romans 8:5–8,13–14

Only by following the Spirit is there life.

V. **Sectarianism is a manifestation of the flesh.**

Galatians 5:19–21 (KJV)

Seditions and heresies (or factions, NASB) are the work of the flesh. These works of the flesh are evident in the sectarianism that divides the Body of Christ. Sedition is an attempt to divide. It is organized rebellion against the authority that God has set in His Church. The word "seditions" is a derivative of the Greek word used to describe Barabbas' crime (Luke 23:19, KJV). Barabbas was cast into prison because of murder and sedition against the Roman government.

VI. **Sectarianism is a sin against the Headship of the Lord Jesus Christ.**

Isaiah 26:12–13

Every organization has its own earthly head. Thus the Church has become a multi-headed monstrosity in the eyes of the world. Every head is warring against the others. Each earthly head usurps the authority that belongs only to Jesus Christ. This results in hatred and strife. It produces **pride and competition** in the Church, which should never be.

VII. **Sectarianism keeps the Church in its infancy by preventing any further revelation.**

Many churches and movements begin with a fresh experience from God that brings new light on the Scriptures. However, after a generation or two, they construct walls around that truth. Regardless of how good their intentions seem to be, organizations, denominations, and sects actually divide the Body of Christ and keep the people in immaturity (I Corinthians 3:1–4). Their sectarianism is supposed to "safeguard" the truth, but it actually fences out further revelation. It is a fact of history that most movements and groups do not open the door to further revelation and light from the Scriptures after becoming organized.

Knowledge and understanding will be ours after we are weaned. The carnal and the babes receive only milk.
Isaiah 28:9

VIII. **Sectarianism holds the world back from believing.**
John 17:20–23

IX. **Only the Holy Spirit and His glory upon us can make us one Body.**
I Corinthians 12:13   John 17:22

Even if every denomination and church group would scrap its charter and come together into one new church organization, **this would not be the coming together of the Body of Christ**. The unity that God wants in His Body is a spiritual unity, "Even as Thou, Father, art in Me, and I in Thee."
John 17:21

X. **Here is the picture of the true unity of the Body of Christ.**
Acts 2:41–47

A.   The fear of the Lord brought a unity.
Acts 5:11–16

B.   Results are promised by unity.
Ephesians 4:16

C.   We are to have one mind.
Philippians 1:27   Philippians 2:4

REVIEW QUESTIONS

1. Explain this statement: "The Church is not a building."

2. Explain this statement: "The Church is not a denomination or a sect."

3. Why is sectarianism a sin against the Headship of Christ over the Church?

4. Do you think that believers will grow better in a church that is under the Lordship of Jesus Christ or in a church under human authority?

5. Do you think a world-church organization could ever bring the Body of Christ together? Why or why not?

The Restoration of the Church

SCRIPTURE READINGS

Acts 3:19–26
Joel 1 and 2
James 5:7–8

Isaiah 61
Malachi 3:1–5
Ephesians 5:26–27

LESSON

I.   **The Church has lost its first love and its first faith.**
Revelation 2:4–5   Jude 3–4   II Peter 2:1–19

II.   **The Apostle Peter spoke of the Lord's coming in connection with the restitution or establishing of all things which the prophets have prophesied.**

The NASB calls this "the restoration of all things."
Acts 3:19–26

III. **Isaiah prophesied the double portion of the Holy Spirit upon God's people to restore and repair the desolations of many generations.**
Isaiah 61:1–7

IV.   **Joel prophesied the destruction and the restoration of God's vineyard.**
Joel 1:3–4,7   Joel 2:23–32

You are God's vineyard (field or husbandry).
I Corinthians 3:9

V.   Malachi foresaw the Lord's purifying of His people so that their worship and service would be pure and perfect, "as in the days of old."

Malachi 3:1–5

This means spiritual restoration.

VI.   The Lord will pour out His Spirit upon His vineyard until the fruit—"the precious fruit of the earth"—matures and is perfect, and then He will come for them.

James 5:7–8 (KJV)

VII.   Then we can be sure that the Lord Jesus Christ will have a Church with the power and purity of the Church in the New Testament.

Ephesians 5:26–27

The Lordship of Jesus Christ

SCRIPTURE READINGS

Ephesians 1:9–11   Colossians 1:12–23
Philippians 2:5–11   Isaiah 11:6–9
I Corinthians 15:20–28   Ephesians 5:22–32
Ephesians 1:15–23   Colossians 2:18–19

LESSON

Jesus is called Savior sixteen times in the New Testament,[1] but He is called Lord seven hundred times.

I.   **The Head of every man is Christ.**

     I Corinthians 11:3

II. **Christ is the Head over all things to the Church.**

     Ephesians 1:15–23   Colossians 1:12–23
     Colossians 2:18–19

III. **Christ is the Head of the Church, which is His Bride.**

     Ephesians 5:22–23,32

IV. **The only basis of genuine union with Christ is subjection to His Headship.**

     Ephesians 5:24

     Members of a headless body are dead. A body with many heads is a monstrosity. Christ must be the Head—the only Head—of the Church.

---

1. Refer to Appendix E.

V. **The Father's eternal purpose is to gather everything in heaven and earth under Christ the Lord.**
Ephesians 1:9–11   Philippians 2:5–11

VI. **Christ is the Lord over nature.**

    A. Over the winds and the sea.
       Matthew 8:26–27

    B. Over the fig tree.
       Matthew 21:19

    C. Over fish.
       Matthew 17:27   John 21:1–12

    D. Over the untamed colt.
       Matthew 21:1–7

    E. Over all things in His Kingdom.
       Isaiah 11:6–9

VII. **Christ shall reign as Lord until all things have been subjected to Him, and then He shall deliver them all unto the Father.**
I Corinthians 15:20–28

CONCLUSION

It is God's will that His Son be the sovereign Lord over every believer, over the Church, over the kingdoms of the world, over all things. The opposition to the Lord's moving in the earth is caused by the resistance of human headship to Christ's Lordship. There is a conflict between human headship that controls the churches and Christ's Headship manifested through the authority of foundational ministries.

Man wants to overrule the Lord. Man wants the glory and the praise that belong to the Lord Jesus Christ alone. Man wants that which gives him pleasure in the Church rather than that which gives the Lord Jesus Christ pleasure.

Submission

SCRIPTURE READINGS

I Samuel 15
James 4:7–8
Ezekiel 2, 3, and 12
Ephesians 5:21—6:9

II Thessalonians 2:7
Isaiah 65:2–6
I Timothy 2:11–15
Isaiah 1:2–9

LESSON

I. **Lawlessness and rebellion will be prevalent in these end times.**

Matthew 7:21–23   Matthew 24:12–13
II Thessalonians 2:7

The word in II Thessalonians 2:7 that is translated in the KJV as "iniquity" means "lawlessness" and "rebellion."

II Timothy 3:1–8   II Peter 2:9–10   Jude 8–10,17–19

II. **Rebellion was severely judged by the Lord.**

A. In the Old Testament, Israel's great sin was rebellion.
Jeremiah 5:23–24   Ezekiel 2, 3, and 12
Isaiah 1:2–9   Isaiah 65:2–6

B. Saul was rejected as king because of rebellion.
I Samuel 15:10–29

C. The prophet Hananiah died for speaking rebellion against the Lord.
Jeremiah 28

D. Shemaiah died childless for speaking rebellion against the Lord.
Jeremiah 29:24–32

III. The Scriptures teach us to be submissive, not rebellious.

A. Submission to authority in the church.
Hebrews 13:17

B. Submission to ministries.
I Corinthians 16:15–16

C. Submission one to another.
Ephesians 5:21   I Peter 5:5–6

D. Submission of a wife to her husband.
Ephesians 5:22–27   Colossians 3:18

E. Submission of children to their parents.
Ephesians 6:1–4   I Timothy 3:4

Note the Old Testament penalty for filial disobedience in Deuteronomy 21:18–21. There were no juvenile delinquents in ancient Israel.

F. Submission of a servant to his master (or employer).
Ephesians 6:5–9   I Peter 2:18–19

G. Submission of woman to man.
I Timothy 2:11–15

H. Submission to the laws of the land and to its rulers.
I Peter 2:13–15   Romans 13:1–8   Titus 3:1

I. Submission to God.
James 4:7–8

  1. Mary's.
    Luke 1:38

  2. Jesus'.
    Matthew 26:39

The word "rebellion" is used often in the Old Testament, but "submission" is rarely used. "Submission" is used often in the New Testament, but "rebellion" is rarely used.

IV.   **The Scriptures teach that all things will be made subject to Christ.**

I Corinthians 15:25–28   Philippians 3:21

Terminology

INTRODUCTION

Some of the scriptural terms used in the lessons in this book may not be familiar to the student. The lessons will be easier to understand if you can acquaint yourself with a few of these terms and their meanings. These terms are arranged in an order which will build in meaning as you progress through the lesson.

LESSON

I.   **The anointing.**

The term "being anointed by the Holy Spirit" refers to anyone speaking or ministering or functioning by the Holy Spirit.

A.   In the Old Testament, oil was poured on the heads of those who were set apart by the prophets of God for a priestly or a kingly office. From that point on, they were set apart unto God for that service and "anointed" to perform that service by the Spirit of God.

Exodus 30:30   I Samuel 16:12–13

B.   In the New Testament, the Holy Spirit was poured out from heaven upon the believers, and they were described as having received an anointing.

I John 2:27

II.   **Tongues.**

Speaking with "new tongues" is one of the signs that Jesus said was to follow the proclaiming of the Word.

Mark 16:17,20

A. The speaking in tongues described in Acts 2 was the speaking in new languages that the believers had never learned, which occurred as they received the Holy Spirit.

Acts 2:1–12

B. I Corinthians 12:10 describes the gift of various kinds of tongues, which is one of the gifts of the Holy Spirit.

C. Abuses of tongues and restrictions upon their use are described in I Corinthians 14.

III. **Prophecy.**

Prophecy is an utterance inspired by the Holy Spirit of truths divinely revealed.

A. In the Bible, prophecy sometimes meant foretelling or predicting events. This form of prophecy is one of the many aspects of the ministry of the prophet.

B. Do not confuse the ministry of the prophet with the gift of prophecy, which is given to members of the Body that they may speak to people to edify, to exhort, and to comfort.

I Corinthians 14

Hence, the prophecies in the services are to be primarily for the building up of the people, and not for the prediction of future happenings.

IV. **The Living Word.**

A. The letter of the Law, and the Scriptures when taught by men devoid of the Holy Spirit, are death and give no life.

II Corinthians 3:6–8

B. The Word of God, illuminated by the Holy Spirit and spoken under the anointing of the Holy Spirit, is living and life-giving.

Hebrews 4:12

C. We speak of the anointed utterance of a Word from God as the "Living Word," because that Word is living and it gives life.

V. The laying on of hands.

A. More than a formality, the laying on of hands is the means by which things of spirit can be transferred or imparted from one person to another.

B. It is one of the means whereby a person may receive healing, the infilling of the Holy Spirit, the gifts of the Spirit, and ordination to a ministry.

Mark 16:18   Acts 19:6   II Timothy 1:6
Acts 13:2–3

VI. To minister.

To minister means to serve or to help another by means of the anointing of the Holy Spirit through some gift of the Spirit, such as a Word of wisdom, faith, the working of miracles, or a gift of healings.

VII. To be ministered to.

This means receiving help or counsel as other believers serve you to meet your need through the anointing of the Holy Spirit.

VIII. A Word.

A. As members of the Body, we can minister strength and encouragement to one another. We can also speak a Word from the Lord to one another. This means that the Holy Spirit gives an individual a

Word of wisdom or a Word of knowledge or a revelation concerning another person (I Corinthians 12:7–8), and that individual speaks the Word to that person.

B. Great restraint should be shown when giving someone a Word which you believe is from the Lord. It is always best to minister to a person in the presence of established ministries in the church who can confirm whether or not that Word is from the Lord.[1] Many difficulties and much confusion are avoided by ministering in authorized groups rather than privately.

IX. **The presence of the Lord.**

The term "presence of the Lord" is a literal translation of the Greek word *parousia*. The *parousia* is a period of time during which the Lord will manifest Himself to His people.

A. This word *parousia* is often mistranslated in Bible versions as the "coming" of the Lord.

Matthew 24:3,27,37–39

1. The word "presence" indicates an extended period of time in which He is revealed and works His will.

2. In contrast, the word "coming" implies that all of the things prophesied for the *parousia* will be done more or less instantaneously.

3. This latter viewpoint has led to much confusion about the prophetic events of the last days.

---

1. Refer to Lesson 48, items IV, B and IV, D.

B. The Lord promised to do many things during His presence in the last days.

I Thessalonians 3:13   I Thessalonians 5:23
II Thessalonians 2:8

X. The Church.

The word "church" is translated from the Greek word *ekklesia*, meaning "that which is called out."

A. The New Testament gives us this picture: the Church is the Body of Jesus Christ; He is the sole Head.

Colossians 1:18   Ephesians 1:22

B. The Church is not a building or a denomination or an organization. Rather, it is a spiritual body of believers set apart to serve the Lord.

XI. The local church.

The term "local church" designates a group of believers in a certain locality who gather to worship and to minister to one another according to the scriptural pattern for the church.

A. The local church is a free, Spirit–filled body of people, governed and united under the Lordship of Jesus Christ according to the New Testament's instructions for the local churches.

B. The local church is not a sect; it is not a division of the Body of Christ. The local church represents a portion of the Body of Christ in a specific area.

XII. Babylon.

A. The people of Babel had an idolatrous religion. In their pride and arrogance, they sought to make a name for themselves in defiance of God. When God confused their language and scattered them, they

spread that confusion throughout the world. Thus, Babel was the origin of religious confusion.
Genesis 11:1–9

B. Babylon as described in Revelation 17 and 18 is a symbol of the idolatrous, sectarian aspects of Christianity, a source of confusion and unfaithfulness to the Lord Jesus Christ.

C. This picture of Babylon is in contrast to the true Church, the Bride of Christ presented in Revelation 19.

XIII. Submission.

Submission is accepting the authority of another. Submission is being open and obedient to those who are over you in the Lord.

A. Submission does not mean that you are inferior to the one you are submissive to. True submission is the avenue by which God's authority is conveyed to His people. It provides the freedom to move in all that God has for you.
Luke 7:6–10

B. The New Testament presents the pattern for submission to divinely appointed authority in the home and in the church.
Ephesians 4:7–16   Ephesians 5:21–27
Ephesians 6:1–4   Hebrews 13:17   I Peter 5:1–5

XIV. Rebellion.

Rebellion is resistance to authority, or defiance of authority.

A. The spiritual condition of rebellion is the problem of this age.
II Timothy 3:1–5

B.   Rebellion also seems to be the greatest problem in the lives of God's people, hindering their walking in a true ministry before the Lord.

XV.   Gifts of the Spirit.

These gifts are endowments of the grace of God upon individual Spirit-filled believers.

A.   By these gifts, believers minister and serve the other members of the Body of Christ.

I Corinthians 12:7–11

B.   The gifts are also the means by which we minister to the world.

Acts 8:5–8

XVI.   Apostolic ministry, prophetic ministry.

A.   The ministries of the apostle and the prophet are the foundational ministries of the Church.

Ephesians 2:19–22

B.   Often the functioning and manifestation of the apostolic and prophetic ministries are found in those who will later be designated by the Spirit to be apostles and prophets, although there may be only a partial expression at present.

XVII.   Impartation.

Impartation is the bestowing on another of a share or a portion of that which God has given to you.

A.   Paul said that he longed to impart spiritual gifts to the Roman Christians.

Romans 1:11

B.   God is raising up ministries today who can impart to other believers that which God has given them.

II Timothy 2:2

XVIII. In the wilderness.

This term is taken from the experiences of the Israelites, who were forced to go through a proving in the wilderness before they were allowed by God to go into their inheritance in the land of Canaan.

Deuteronomy 8:2

A. Jesus also was tempted in the wilderness before He entered into His ministry.

Mark 1:11–15

B. Those who receive personal prophecies and are commissioned to a ministry usually go through a time of testing which we sometimes refer to as a "wilderness experience."

XIX. To ordain a ministry.

To ordain a ministry is to appoint a person to fulfill a specific function in the church, such as an elder, a deacon, an apostle, a prophet, a pastor, or other ministry designated by the Spirit.

A. Ordination is usually accomplished with the laying on of hands and prophetic confirmation. This occurs after a period of time in which the individual has been set aside for the ministry and has gone through testing.

B. Remember that a ministry is God-given, not man-given.

XX. The Kingdom of God.

God's Kingdom has always been a spiritual kingdom, "not of this world."

John 18:36

A. In these days the truths of the Kingdom of God are being particularly emphasized by the Holy Spirit, for the Kingdom of God is to fill the whole earth in the days ahead of us.

B. "The kingdom of this world will become the Kingdom of our Lord and of His Christ."
Revelation 11:15

XXI. The Sabbath.

A. The Lord is bringing new light on the scriptural teaching of the Sabbath. This is the Sabbath that is related to God's Kingdom, where we cease from our labors and striving, and we enter into His rest.
Hebrews 4

B. The keeping of the Sabbath is an expression of anticipation and faith in the coming of the Lord in His Kingdom.
Isaiah 56:1–2   Isaiah 58:13–14

C. For a number of years at the beginning of the Church, believers observed both the Sabbath and the first day of the week.
Acts 16:13   Acts 20:7

XXII. The feasts.

A. The Lord is restoring the spiritual observance of the feasts that Israel was commanded to keep.[2,3]
Exodus 23:14–16   Deuteronomy 16:16–17

It is scriptural to observe the feasts; they are times of gathering inaugurated by the Lord. In our celebration, we rejoice in the spiritual fulfillment that has

---

2. JOHN RITCHIE, *Feasts of Jehovah* (Grand Rapids, MI: Kregel Publications, 1982).
3. GEORGE H. WARNOCK, *The Feast of Tabernacles: The Hope of the Church* (Cranbrook, B.C., Canada: George H. Warnock, 1951).

already occurred, and we anticipate the fulfillment that is yet to come.

B. The early Church continued to observe the feasts.

Acts 2:1   Acts 18:21, KJV   Acts 20:16
I Corinthians 5:7–8   I Corinthians 16:8

C. The prophet Zechariah prophesied that the Feast of Tabernacles would be observed in the Kingdom.

Zechariah 14:9,16–19

XXIII. Discernment.

Discernment is insight or understanding given by the Holy Spirit into matters that may be hidden.

A. God gives the ability to discern between good and evil.

Hebrews 5:14   Malachi 3:18   Ezekiel 44:23

B. Discernment is necessary for governing God's people wisely.

I Kings 3:9–12   I Chronicles 12:1,32

C. God gives discernment to His people so they may understand the times.

Daniel 9:22   Daniel 12:3,10

D. Discernment is also given to bring spiritual penetration into the underlying problems, bondages, or oppressions of people.

E. Discernment may be given through the Word of wisdom, through the Word of knowledge, or through the gift of discerning of spirits.

I Corinthians 12:8–10

XXIV. Revelation.

Revelation is the communication by God of His will and truths to man.

A. The prophets received the revelations from God that constitute the Bible.

I Peter 1:10–12   II Peter 1:20–21

B. God is still showing His will and His truths to man.

I Corinthians 2:6–13

XXV. Illumination.

A. Illumination is the enlightenment that the Holy Spirit gives concerning the Word of God.

B. The Holy Spirit may reveal a truth to one; and as that one declares the truth to others, the Holy Spirit then illuminates that truth to them so that they also may understand it.

XXVI. The restoration of all things.

A. The term "the Restoration" is commonly used to describe God bringing the Church back to its condition and glory as described in the book of Acts.

Acts 3:21

B. The correct meaning of Acts 3:21 is "until the time for the establishing of all those things of which God has spoken by the mouth of all His holy prophets." What God is doing today is more than a restoration of the early Church. He is establishing His Kingdom on earth, as prophesied by every prophet from Samuel onward, through the ministry of a Church restored to its New Testament glory and beyond.

Ephesians 1:9–10   I Corinthians 2:9

XXVII. The glory of the Lord.

The glory of the Lord is the manifestation of God's presence and splendor to the spiritual and physical faculties of man.

A. When the prophets prophesied that God's temple in the last days would have greater glory than the glory that was seen in Solomon's temple, they meant that God's presence would be revealed to the heart of man, and also to his eyesight.

I Kings 8:10–11   Haggai 2:9   Isaiah 4:5–6

B. God's glory will be visited upon His people.

Daniel 12:3   II Corinthians 3:17–18

XXVIII. Vision.

A. God says that He reveals Himself to the prophet by a vision or a dream.

Numbers 12:6

B. Old Testament prophets were sometimes called "seers" because of this faculty of spiritual sight. The realm of spirit actually became visible to many of them.

II Kings 6:15–17   Daniel 1:17

C. This spiritual sight will be given to many of God's servants in these days.

XXIX. The spirit realm.

A. The spirit realm is the realm of spirit beings, such as angels, demons, and Satan, as well as God and Christ our Savior.

B. It is in this spirit realm that our great struggles and our great victories take place.

Ephesians 6:10–12

XXX. The leading of the Lord.

A. God's servants were always led and directed by the Holy Spirit as to what they were to do and to say.

Genesis 24:48   Acts 8:25–29

B.   Today God is raising up a people who will be led by the Holy Spirit in everything they do or say.

Romans 8:14   Luke 12:11–12

XXXI. First Principles.

This term is used to describe the foundational, fundamental teachings of the Scriptures which every believer should know.

Hebrews 5:12, KJV

XXXII. A walk in the Spirit.

To live a life that is directed by the Holy Spirit and to live in constant awareness of the presence of the Lord should be the objective of every believer. To live this way is to walk in the Spirit.

A.   The condition of your spirit is more important than anything else about you.

B.   Your spirit must be open to know and accept the Lordship of Jesus Christ over you.

XXXIII. Worship.

Worship is a spiritual veneration, adoration, exaltation, and reverence of the Lord God, accompanied by thanksgiving and praise to Him.

A.   God is looking for true worshipers who will worship Him in spirit and in truth.

John 4:19–24

B.   Worship is not form or ritual. It is more than thanksgiving, praise, and singing.

C.   True worship is from the heart.

XXXIV. Singing in the Spirit.

A. This is singing before the Lord under the anointing and inspiration of the Holy Spirit.
   I Corinthians 14:15

B. This is not singing from a hymnal. Singing in the Spirit is an inspired and anointed utterance by the Holy Spirit.

XXXV. The Lordship of Christ.

A. Christ Jesus is to be our Lord.
   Philippians 2:9–11

B. He is our Head in everything.
   Colossians 1:16–18

C. In these days the Spirit is emphasizing His Lordship over our lives. We are experiencing the dethronement of self and the ending of man-rule so that Christ might be our only Lord.

XXXVI. The flesh.

The flesh is the bodily nature, as distinguished from the spiritual nature.

A. The New Testament speaks of the flesh as the old nature which is full of disobedience to the Lord.
   Romans 8:5–8

B. The word "carnal" is another term used to refer to the flesh nature.

XXXVII. Soulish.

This word describes that which is of the human soul: the emotions, the will, the intellect. Much religious effort is born in the soulish realm of man, not in the realm of his spirit. Hence, the Word of God comes to us to divide between soul and spirit.

Hebrews 4:12

XXXVIII. Signs of the Spirit.

A. Many of God's people today experience signs, or indications in their physical body, given by the Holy Spirit.

Romans 8:11

B. We do not follow such signs; they follow us as we are doing the will of God.

Mark 16:15–17,20, KJV

New Testament Tithing and Giving

SCRIPTURE READINGS

Hebrews 7
II Corinthians 8 and 9
I Corinthians 16:1–4

INTRODUCTION

The purpose of this lesson is to show the New Testament basis of tithing, the ministry of giving, and the grace of God that rests on people to give.

LESSON

I.   **Tithing.**

Hebrews 7

   A. Abraham tithed to Melchizedek, king of Jerusalem and priest of God. Was Melchizedek Shem? an angel? God? Christ? Yes, He was Christ.

Hebrews 7:1–2

   B. Melchizedek was "without father or mother," i.e., not holding priesthood by lineage.

Hebrews 7:3   Genesis 14:17–20

   C. Tithing principles are operative to Christ as priest according to the order of Melchizedek. Our tithing is not based on the Levitical law of tithing.

Hebrews 7:4–10

D. The Levitical priesthood did not bring perfection.
Hebrews 7:11–12

E. Christ's priesthood is an unchanging priesthood.
Hebrews 7:13–17

F. Christ's priesthood is an eternal priesthood.
Hebrews 7:18–24

God has fulfilled the old covenant and has given us a
new covenant and a new priesthood (Hebrews 8:7–13).
Thus, we tithe under the new covenant and we tithe
to the Lord Jesus Christ, who is of the new priesthood after the order of Melchizedek.

II. **Giving.**

II Corinthians 8 and 9

Tithes are the tenth of our increase due to God. Offerings
are our worship gifts to God. Alms are our gifts to the
poor and needy.

Paul and other ministries took the offering for the saints
at Jerusalem described in II Corinthians 8 and 9. It was a
large collection, requiring over a year to gather.

Paul had spent years preaching to the Gentiles not to be
Jewish proselytes, and now they were showing their love
to the Jewish Christians. This shows the unity and love of
the Church in the New Testament. It was one of the great
events of the New Testament.

A. How the Macedonians gave.
II Corinthians 8:1–5

B. Titus collected the offering from the Corinthian
church.
II Corinthians 8:6

C. Giving is by the grace of God.
II Corinthians 8:7

D. Giving is a test of love.
II Corinthians 8:8–9

E. Giving is based on what you have to give.
II Corinthians 8:10–12

F. Giving is to be equally shared by all saints.
II Corinthians 8:13–15

G. The gathering and administration of the giving is to be irreproachable.
II Corinthians 8:16–24

H. Advance notice was given so that the people could save and set aside something to give.
II Corinthians 9:1–5

I. Giving is to be bountiful (the law of harvest).
II Corinthians 9:6

J. Giving is to be with the heart. This brings God's special love.
II Corinthians 9:7

K. There is a ministry of faith and grace in giving.
II Corinthians 9:8–10

L. Giving contributes to worship and praise to God.
II Corinthians 9:11–12

M. The giving of the Gentile Christians caused the Jerusalem Christians to praise God for them.
II Corinthians 9:13–15

Chastening and Testing

SCRIPTURE READINGS

Hebrews 12:1–17
I Peter 4
I Peter 1:6–8
II Corinthians 4, 10, and 11

LESSON

I.   Chastening and discipline in the life of a believer are evident tokens of his sonship and of God's love.

Hebrews 12:6–8

II.   Chastening and discipline bring God's holiness and the fruit of righteousness in the believer's life.

Hebrews 12:9–11

III. Reproaches and sufferings for Christ have a real purpose.

I Peter 4:1–7,13–19

IV.   Sufferings in the lives of the ministries will result in the glory of God resting upon them.

I Peter 4:12–14

V.   Tests and trials have a real purpose in our lives.

James 1:2–4   I Peter 1:6–7   II Corinthians 4:17

VI.   How the ministries suffer and are tested.

II Corinthians 4, 10, and 11

VII. Our attitude toward trials, temptations, persecutions, and chastening is not to be that of grumbling or whining, but of rejoicing.

James 1:2–4   I Peter 1:6–8   I Peter 4:10–19
Matthew 5:10–12   Luke 6:22–23   Hebrews 10:32–34

MEAT
FOR THE
YOUNG MEN

A General Survey of the Body of Christ

SCRIPTURE READING

Ephesians 4

LESSON

I. **The unity and spirit in the Church.**
    Ephesians 4:1-6

    A. The first truth is the oneness of the Body of Christ. Verses 2 and 3 reveal the only spirit that can prevail in the members if Body ministry is to work.

    B. What is Body ministry?

        It is the Christ-exalting and Christ-directed spiritual ministry of the Church, the Body of Christ, as God enables each member.
        Verses 4-6

II. **The gifts (endowments) by grace for the Church.**
    Ephesians 4:7-10

    A. God gives grace to each member according to the measure of Christ's gift to him.

    B. All the ministries in the Body of Christ and all the gifts of the Spirit are endowments of the grace of God.

    C. The end of all ministry—its divine purpose—is that Christ might fill all things. Everything must end in Him.

III. **The gift-ministries for the Church and their function.**
Ephesians 4:11–12

    A. The gift-ministries are apostles, prophets, evangelists, pastors and teachers.

    B. What is their function?

    They are to equip the saints for the work of service, so that the Body of Christ can build itself up.

IV. **The objectives of the gift-ministries in the Church.**
Ephesians 4:13–16

    A. The objectives are outlined in verse 13.

        1. Until we all attain to the unity of the faith.

        2. Until we attain to the knowledge of the Son of God.

        3. Until we attain to maturity, to the measure of the stature of the fullness of Christ.

    B. The development and establishing of the individual believer is outlined in verse 14.

        1. That we may not be children.

        2. That we may not be tossed to and fro.

        3. That we may not be carried about:

            a. By every wind of doctrine.

            b. By the trickery of men.

            c. By craftiness in deceitful scheming.

C. The development and coordination of the Body of Christ is shown in verses 15–16.

But speaking the truth in love, we are to grow up in all aspects into Him, who is the head, even Christ, from whom the whole body, being fitted and held together by that which every joint supplies, according to the proper working of each individual part, causes the growth of the body for the building up of itself in love.

This is how perfection comes forth in the Body of Christ.

V. **This is the general survey of the Body of Christ.**

A. Note that Ephesians 4:17—6:9 gives various careful instructions for our walk, emphasizing the spirit we are to have and manifest toward one another in every relationship of our lives.

B. Studying Ephesians 4 gives us the general picture of the Body of Christ. Other lessons deal with specific phases of what God is restoring today to His Body, the Church.

Ministries

SCRIPTURE READINGS

Romans 12
Ephesians 4
I Corinthians 12 and 13

LESSON

I. **A ministry depends upon Christ, not upon man.**
    Romans 12:1–6

    A. You present your body a sacrifice to God by His mercies.
        Verse 1

    B. You receive the mind of Christ, in order that you may know God's will for you.
        Verse 2

    C. Esteem for yourself the ministry that comes from the assigned measure of faith that God has given you.
        Verse 3

    D. Our function in the Body of Christ and our gifts differ and depend upon the grace that God gives us.
        Verses 4–6. See also I Corinthians 7:7.

    These verses show that we enter a consecration of our bodies through His mercies; we find God's will for us through Christ's mind; we take our place of ministry through a measure of faith which Christ gives us; and we fill a distinct function in the Body of Christ by the grace that He gives to us. Therefore, a ministry depends upon His mercies, His mind, His will, His faith, and His grace!

II. **There are seven general classifications of ministries.**
Romans 12:6–8

The ministry gifts of Christ are given to fulfill assigned ministries, and we must use them accordingly. See also Ephesians 4:7, 15–16.

A. Prophecy—in proportion to our faith.

B. Service—use this gift in serving others.

C. Teaching—use this gift in teaching.

D. Exhortation—use this gift in exhorting (for example, encouragement, introducing people to Christ, teaching).

E. Giving—with liberality.

F. Leading—with diligence (that is, with moral earnestness).

G. Showing mercy—with cheerfulness.

These seven phases or distinctions, as given in Romans 12:6–8, are general classifications of the ministries. Every believer should have a ministry in one or more of these general classifications.

III. **Many specific ministries are included in these general classifications.**

A. Prophecy—includes apostles, prophets, evangelists, pastors and teachers, singers of psalms, and any ministry who moves in the gift of prophecy.

B. Service—includes deacons and deaconesses (both temporal and spiritual service to the Body), ministries of helps (may include publishing and clerical work, janitorial work, maintenance and repair work).

C. Teaching—includes elders, deacons, Bible teachers, teachers of children, and many others.

D. Exhortation—includes introducing people to Christ, Bible teaching, testifying, exhorting in the services, giving encouragement.

E. Giving—includes working of miracles, gift of faith, hospitality, ministry of giving.

F. Leading, or ruling—includes apostles, prophets, pastors, elders, and others who are commissioned to lead or direct.

G. Showing mercy—includes the elder ministry, visiting and praying for the sick, helping the poor, caring for orphans and widows.

No ministry is assumed; it is assigned by the Lord. We must not seek a place or refuse to fill the place that God gives us. These seven phases of Christ's endowment of ministries in the Body of Christ are found in varying combinations, according to the proportion of the grace and faith given to each ministry.

IV. **Several basic ministries and offices in the Body of Christ are specifically named in Ephesians 4 and I Corinthians 12.**

A. Ephesians 4:11–16   I Corinthians 12:27–31

1. Apostles.

2. Prophets.

3. Evangelists.

4. Pastors and teachers.

5. Miracles.

6. Gifts of healings.

7. Helps.

8. Gifts of administration.

9. Various kinds of tongues.

B. Apostles and prophets are the foundational ministries, and others build on their foundation (Ephesians 2:19–22; I Corinthians 3:6–10).

V. **Very important instructions about the path of love that the ministries must follow are included in each of these chapters on the ministries.**

Romans 12:9–21   I Corinthians 12:27—13:13
Ephesians 4:15–32

VI. **After God assigns each one a ministry, He sends the fire to try him.**

I Peter 4:10–19

VII. **Are the gifts of the Holy Spirit ministries?**

Not necessarily. You cannot have a ministry without a gift of the Spirit, but you may have a gift without having a ministry. The believer who walks in a gift faithfully, humbly, led by the Spirit and not by self-ambition, will find his gift becoming a ministry. A gift is an endowment of the Holy Spirit. A ministry is a specific function of Christ in His Body.

VIII. **Intercessory prayer should be a part of every ministry.**
Ephesians 6:18

A. Paul engaged in prayer for the churches continually.
Ephesians 1:15–16   Romans 1:9   Philippians 1:4
Colossians 1:3   I Thessalonians 1:2

B. The twelve apostles also were devoted to prayer.
Acts 6:4

Usually intercession is not a ministry by itself; it is the means by which **all ministries** function, from Christ the Head (Hebrews 7:25) to the smallest and weakest ministry.

IX. **Are the ministries to be supported?**

Often a ministry in the New Testament worked with his hands and supported himself, unless he was an elder or a ministry who devoted himself full time to laboring in the Word and teaching, in which case he was to be adequately supported.

II Thessalonians 3   I Timothy 5:17–18   I Corinthians 9

The New Testament Church Pattern

SCRIPTURE READINGS

Acts 13 and 14
I Timothy 4:12–16
II Timothy 1:6–7
Ephesians 4:10–16
Romans 1:9–15
I Corinthians 4
Titus 1:4–11
I Timothy 3
I Peter 5:1–10

Ephesians 2:19–22
I Corinthians 1:4–10
I Corinthians 10:1–6
I Corinthians 12 and 14
I Timothy 5:17–22
I Timothy 1:18–19
Romans 12:3–8
Hebrews 2:1–4

LESSON

I. **How the ministries are ordained and sent forth to lay the foundations of the churches.**

   Acts 13:1–5

   A. Note the list given here of prophets and teachers in the church at Antioch.

   B. See how devoted they were to prayer, fasting, and ministering to the Lord.

   C. Note that the Holy Spirit is the director of the work of the church.

   D. After fasting, hands were laid on the ministries and they were sent forth.

   E. Barnabas and Saul were among the prophets and teachers named in Acts 13:1; but they were ordained and sent forth to lay foundations, and so they were called "apostles" in Acts 14:14.

II. **How the local churches are to be started.**
Acts 14:7–23,27

    A.   The gospel is preached and believed.
         Verse 7

    B.   Miracles confirm the Word of God.
         Verses 8–10

    C.   The apostles are misunderstood and persecuted.
         Verses 11–20

    D.   There is encouragement through trials.
         Verse 22

    E.   They ordain elders in the local churches.
         Verse 23

    F.   After fasting and praying, they leave them in God's hands.
         Verse 23

    G.   The apostles come back and report to the home church.
         Verse 27

    H.   Later, they return to see how the churches are doing.
         Acts 15:36,40–41

III. **How the local churches are directed and fed and grow up to perfection under the foundational ministries.**
Ephesians 4:10–16   Ephesians 2:19–22

The apostle and the prophet are given to equip the church so that it can be perfected. (The other gift-ministries are the evangelist, and the pastor and teacher.)

    A.   The apostle imparts and establishes.
         Romans 1:9–15

B.   The local church should be complete with all the gifts and ministries. Note that some of the gift-ministries may travel throughout various churches and are not necessarily resident in one specific local church.
   I Corinthians 1:4–9

C.   The apostle's ministry is confirmed by signs and wonders and the distribution of spiritual gifts.
   Hebrews 2:1–4

D.   See the deep concern, the authority, and the power of the "father" ministry in the church.
   II Corinthians 12:12   II Corinthians 13:1–3
   II Corinthians 10:1–6   I Corinthians 4:9–21

IV.   **How the local churches are governed and directed.**

A.   Paul sent Titus to:

   1.   Set in order things lacking in the church.

   2.   Appoint elders according to the qualifications given by Paul.
      Titus 1:4–11

B.   More about elders and bishops (overseers).
   I Timothy 3:1–7   I Timothy 5:17–22   I Peter 5:1–10

C.   The functions of deacons.

   The deacon is a ministry of service. Deacons serve the spiritual and temporal needs of the Body as directed by the Holy Spirit.
   I Timothy 3:8–13   Acts 6:1–6

   1.   Deacons are to be full of the Spirit and of wisdom.

2. In the early Church, deacons performed miracles, prophesied, taught, evangelized, healed the sick, and preached the Gospel.

    Acts 6:8–10   Acts 8:5–8,12–13,26–40

3. In the day-to-day ministry to the local church, deacons are to be involved in all aspects of teaching related to the church and the families, including setting a home in order on the natural level, creating a spiritual home, and managing finances.

V. **How the local churches are endowed with gifts of the Holy Spirit.**

A. The gifts of the Holy Spirit.
    I Corinthians 12:4–11

B. How are these gifts given?
    I Timothy 4:12–16   II Timothy 1:6–7

C. Personal prophecies may come to reveal what gifts and ministries are in the plan of God for an individual.
    I Timothy 1:18–19

VI. **How the local churches are endowed with ministries.**
    Romans 12:3–8   I Corinthians 12:14–31

VII. **How the local churches are to conduct their services.**
    I Corinthians 14

A. These verses describe the worship service.
    Verses 15,26–31

B. Prophecy is preferred to tongues.
    Verses 4–6,23–25

C. One hard and fast rule for the services: everything must be done to edify.

Verses 12,26

REVIEW QUESTIONS

1. Are apostles to be sent out by missionary boards or denominations to start churches? Explain.

2. Which ministries are especially endowed to equip the church so that it can be perfected?

3. Can you name the nine gifts of the Spirit?

4. Name the ministries in the local body of believers.

5. What are the qualifications of an elder? of a deacon?

6. What should be in the church services, according to I Corinthians 14?

7. Do you think we have seen much of the "father" ministry in the churches as Paul described it?

8. What is the pattern for the reception and revelation of the gifts of the Holy Spirit for the individual believer?

9. Do you think the church has followed the scriptural pattern described in this lesson? Discuss.

Babylon

SCRIPTURE READINGS

Genesis 10:8–12; 11:1–9 Revelation 18
Isaiah 14:3–23 Revelation 19:1–16
Jeremiah 51 Revelation 21
Revelation 17 Revelation 22:1–7

INTRODUCTION

In this lesson we trace the influence of Babylon as it has come down through the centuries. Babylon is the Greek word for Babel, which means "confusion." It was at Babel where man's languages were confused, and from there idolatry and corruption spread through all the earth. Throughout the Scriptures, Babylon has represented opposition to God's will and the defilement of God's people. The outcries of the prophets against Babylon display God's hatred of Babylon and identify the satanic force that is behind it. Revelation 17 and 18 present the picture of "Babylon the Great, the mother of harlots and of all the abominations of the earth" (Revelation 17:5). In contrast, Revelation 19 portrays the pure Bride of Christ, and tells of the ultimate destruction of Babylon and all that is associated with it.

As we study what the Scriptures and history teach us about Babylon, we must ask ourselves this question: to what extent have our Christian beliefs and traditions been influenced by Babylon? Let us examine our own hearts, not to evaluate doctrines, but to let the Holy Spirit reveal the truth about the extent to which the spirit of Babylon has affected Christianity.

LESSON

I.   **The origin of Babylon.**

    A.   Nimrod founded Babel in the third generation after Noah. The Scriptures say that he became "a mighty one in the earth." This term "mighty one" is the same Hebrew word used to describe the giants, or Nephilim, in Genesis 6:4.[1] Strong's Concordance translates this term as "warrior, tyrant." Nimrod was a strong ruler who built many great cities after the Flood, the first of which was Babel.[2]

       Genesis 10:8–12

    B.   The construction of Babel included the building of a tower which was dedicated to an idolatrous worship. The people at that time had one language and were in agreement on building the city and the tower in order "to make a name for themselves." In response, God confused their language and scattered them over the whole earth.

       Genesis 11:1–9

    C.   This picture of open rebellion to the Lord and His judgment upon the spirit of Babylon is reflected throughout the rest of the Scriptures. After Nimrod, Babylon continued as a great city for many centuries through to Nebuchadnezzar, the Chaldean king who reigned from 605–562 B.C. During that period, the influence of Babylon spread throughout the ancient world (Jeremiah 51:7).

---

1. FINIS JENNINGS DAKE, *Dake's Annotated Reference Bible* (Lawrenceville, GA: Dake Bible Sales, Inc., 1963), 9.
2. JOHN MCCLINTOCK AND JAMES STRONG, ed., *Cyclopedia of Biblical, Theological, and Ecclesiastical Literature* (n.p.: Harper & Brothers, 1867-1877; reprint Grand Rapids, MI: Baker Book House, 1981), s.v. "Nimrod."

D. In the time of Nebuchadnezzar, Babylon was a city of mighty fortresses and great splendor. It was roughly 11 miles square, or 44 miles in circumference. Ancient historians say that its walls were about 300 feet high and wide enough for a six-lane highway on top.[3,4] Diodorus wrote that one of its idols, made of hammered gold, was 40 feet high.[5] The book of Daniel also describes a golden idol in Babylon that was 90 feet tall and 9 feet wide (Daniel 3:1).

E. Under Nebuchadnezzar, Babylon became the dominant political and religious power in the world. Like Nimrod, Nebuchadnezzar assumed a place of greatness that belongs only to God. Daniel wrote that Nebuchadnezzar could command the nations how and what to worship (Daniel 3:3–7). Later, God severely judged Nebuchadnezzar for his arrogance (Daniel 4:29–33).

F. This same arrogance against the Lord appeared in Belshazzar, Nebuchadnezzar's grandson. God not only judged him, but He removed sovereignty from the Chaldeans and turned the kingdom over to the Medes and Persians in 539 B.C. (Daniel 5:22–31; Jeremiah 51:11). Eventually, the ancient city of Babylon became a desolate ruin (Jeremiah 51:37).

II. **The progression of spiritual Babylon to pagan Rome.**

A. During the time of the Babylonian and Persian empires, Asia Minor served as a bridge between those cultures of the east and the Greek and Roman

---

3. HENRY H. HALLEY, *Halley's Bible Handbook*, 24th ed. (Grand Rapids, MI: Zondervan Publishing House, 1965), 336.
4. *The New Unger's Bible Dictionary*, 1988 ed. (Chicago: Moody Press, 1988), s.v. "Babylon," 135.
5. DIODORUS, *The Library of History*, bk. 2, chap. 9, par. 5-9.

cultures of the west. Many of the Greek and Roman deities were patterned after the Babylonian gods.

B.   One of the greatest cities of Asia Minor was Pergamos. The kings of Pergamos ruled much of Asia Minor and presided over one of the greatest centers of pagan cults and idolatrous religions in the world.[6,7]

C.   Attalus III, the last king of Pergamos, bequeathed his kingdom to Rome in 133 B.C.[8] As part of the Roman empire, Pergamos continued to function as an influential authority in religious matters. Revelation 2:12–13 refers to Pergamos as "Satan's throne."

D.   In 74 B.C., Julius Caesar became a pontiff (priest). In 63 B.C., he became the supreme pontiff, or Pontifex Maximus, of the pagan Roman religions.[9] Each emperor after Julius Caesar (until Gratian) took the title Pontifex Maximus, which gave him authority over all pagan religions in the empire. Now the power of the state was combined with the priesthood to enforce religion, just as it was in Babylon with Nebuchadnezzar.

E.   Rome became the center of religious headship and dominion. The book of Revelation clearly identifies Rome, the city on seven hills, as spiritual Babylon[10] (Revelation 17:7,9).

---

6. McClintock and Strong, s.v. "Pergamos," 947–948.
7. Halley, 696.
8. Hermann Kinder and Werner Hilgeman, *The Anchor Atlas of World History*, vol. 1 (Garden City, NY: Anchor Press and Doubleday, 1974), 69.
9. *Encyclopedia Britannica*, 1972 ed., s.v. "Caesar," 574.
10. James Orr, ed., *The International Standard Bible Encyclopedia* (Grand Rapids, MI: Wm. B. Eerdmans Publishing Co., 1976), s.v. "Babylon in the NT."

III. The early Church.

Christ came in the days when the Roman emperors were firmly established and Israel was under their authority. Many of Jesus' followers believed that He would directly confront and overthrow the political and military power of the Roman Empire (John 18:36; Acts 1:6). Instead, He confronted and defeated all the rulers and powers in the spirit realm (Colossians 2:10,15). He redeemed man's relationship with the Father and opened up a spiritual walk with God (John 4:23–24; Ephesians 1:3).

A. Following Christ's death and resurrection, His disciples in obedience stayed together and received the promise of the Spirit (Acts 1:4–5). The Body of Christ, His Church, was born and began to function together in Jerusalem.

Acts 2:42–47

1. The early believers lived in oneness and in an awareness of the Lord. They continually devoted themselves to their relationships with the apostolic Word, with one another, and with the Lord.

As a result, the early Church was filled with power, joy, and worship, and new believers were drawn into their midst daily.

2. The early Christians, being Jews, continued to go to the temple and to minister to the people of Jerusalem.

Acts 2:46; 3:1; 4:13–20; 5:42

3. They kept their focus on the Lord and on the Word. When needs or conflicts arose in the Church, the apostles looked to the Lord and got a Word from God as to how to solve the problem.

Acts 6:1–6

B. As a result of persecution triggered by the stoning of Stephen, those early believers were scattered to other cities (Acts 8:1–4). Eventually, churches were established in many countries, all directed by apostolic authority under the leading of the Holy Spirit.

C. God opening the way for the Gentiles to come into the Church is an example of how the early believers followed the leading of the Spirit.

1. For fifteen years, the Church was made up entirely of Jewish believers. Then God led Cornelius, a Roman centurion, to seek out Peter, while at the same time He was showing Peter that He was opening the door to the Gentiles (Acts 10).

2. Circumcision of the Gentiles soon became an issue which threatened to cause division in the Church. Acts 15 tells how the apostles, prophets, and elders of the Church gathered together and sought the mind of the Lord on the matter. Everyone presented their views; but when the Holy Spirit spoke through James, they all recognized that it was the Lord speaking and gave themselves to it.

IV. **Christianity gradually becomes part of the Roman Empire.**

A. By the end of the first century, the Church had begun to fall away from the apostolic foundation. We see in III John 9–10 that leaders of individual churches, out of their ambition for power, had begun to refuse the apostolic Word and to refuse fellowship with the apostles who had opened the door to Christ for them. John also wrote that the spirit of antichrist had already manifested itself in the churches (II John 7–11). Jude gave similar warnings to the Church (Jude 3–4).

The early apostles were always on guard to protect the believers from being robbed of the simplicity of their faith in Christ (II Corinthians 11:3; I Thessalonians 3:5).

B.   The next two centuries were a period of great growth for Christianity, accompanied by waves of intense persecution. There were many who contended to maintain the pure ministry of Christ. However, as pagan and philosophical influences crept in, the Church began to be divided over various issues. Instead of seeking the mind of the Lord together as the early Church had done, they began to rely on man's thinking.

C.   The influences against the Church were tremendous. Some of the corrupting ideas that became incorporated into Christianity during this time included the following:[11]

1.   The distinction between the clergy and the ordinary believer, with the clergy divided into a strict hierarchy and the believer excluded from performing any ecclesiastical function.

2.   The belief in the merit of external works. These included asceticism (severe treatment of the body), the concept that giving alms could obtain forgiveness of sins, and the perversion of the spiritual ordinances into magical mysteries by which a person could obtain spiritual benefit.

3.   The belief that it is the sole right of the bishop to forgive sins.

4.   The pompous ritualization of the sacraments and the worship service.

---

11. ALBERT HENRY NEWMAN, *A Manual of Church History*, revised and enlarged ed., vol. 1 (Valley Forge, PA: The Judson Press, 1976), 292–293.

By 300 A.D., the churches were very different in lifestyle, teaching, worship, and church order from the churches of 100 A.D.

V.   **Christianity becomes the state religion of the Roman Empire.**

A.   In spite of the persecutions and the corrupting influences, Christianity grew strong and unified beyond any of the pagan religions of the Empire. The emperor Constantine used the strength and unity of Christianity to his advantage. In 313 A.D., he used his authority as Pontifex Maximus to legalize Christianity. He then passed laws that favored Christianity over all other religions with the goal of unifying the Roman empire under himself.[12]

B.   Around 376 A.D., the emperor Gratian refused the title of Pontifex Maximus because of its pagan associations.[13] Shortly thereafter, the emperor Theodosius officially made Christianity the state religion. He specifically decreed that only Christianity as taught by Damasus, the bishop of Rome, was legal.[14] This marked the beginning of the transfer of religious headship from the emperor to the bishop of Rome.

C.   Authority over the Church became more and more centralized in the bishop of Rome. In 455 A.D., the emperor Valentenian III issued a decree that made Leo I the supreme authority in the Church and referred to him as the Pope.[15] The titles "pontiff" and "Pontifex Maximus" began to be applied exclusively to the Pope.

---

12. Ibid., 305–308.
13. Ibid., 310.
14. Theodosian Code 16.1.2.
15. MILTON VIORST, *The Great Documents of Western Civilization* (Philadelphia: Chilton Company, 1965), 18–19.

D. The Dark Ages began in 476 A.D. with the deposing of the last emperor of Rome. This time saw tremendous corruption of the Papacy, with the Pope moving into worldwide political authority. The Church as an organization had fallen away from its spiritual beginnings. It was in this atmosphere that the Restoration eventually began.

   1. In the fourteenth and fifteenth centuries, men such as Wycliffe, Hus, Savonarola, Luther, and Zwingli openly challenged the authority of the Papacy and rejected some of the corrupted doctrines and practices which it promoted. These men brought new light from the Scriptures, and various groups began to split away until the Church was no longer contained under the authority of Rome. This was the beginning of Protestantism.

   2. The sects and denominations of Christianity which have come forth since that time all began with fresh revelation, but they did not continue to seek the Lord for more, as their founders had. Instead, they quickly settled into some form of religious organization and continued in much of the pagan and political influences which they inherited. The Scriptures admonish us still, "Come out of her, My people!" (Revelation 18:4).

VI. **Pagan influences in Christian observances.**

Originally, the early Church celebrated the feasts and followed a manner of worship in accordance with Jewish observances (I Corinthians 5:7–8; Acts 20:16).[16] They recognized the provision of God that the feasts represented and found in Christ the fulfillment of each (Colossians 2:16–17). As time passed, these celebrations

---

16. NEWMAN, vol. 1, 299.

were displaced by pagan observances that were incorporated into Christianity.

A.   Easter.

1.   The early Church celebrated the Passover, worshiping Christ as the true Paschal Lamb (I Corinthians 5:7). The Latin word for "Easter" is *pascha*, which is taken directly from the Greek word for "Passover." In 325 A.D., the Nicean Council established Easter as an observance separate from the Jewish observance of Passover.[17]

2.   The English word "Easter" is a Saxon term for the goddess Estera, to whom sacrifices were offered in April.[18]

3.   The observance of Easter began to take on symbols such as the chicken, decorated eggs, and the bunny, which were also used in pagan Spring rites.[19]

B.   Christmas.

1.   The early Church did not celebrate the birthday of Jesus, and the actual date of His birth is not recorded in the Scriptures. However, many believe that Jesus was born around the time of the Feast of Tabernacles. How did December 25 become designated as the birthday of Christ?

2.   The ante-Nicene father Tertullian (145–220 A.D.) chastised the Christians in his day for celebrating the winter festivals of Saturnalia and

---

17. McClintock and Strong, s.v. "Easter," 13.
18. James Orr, s.v. "Easter."
19. Gertrude Jobes, *Dictionary of Mythology, Folklore, and Symbols* (New York: The Scarecrow Press, Inc., 1961), s.v. "Easter," 487.

New Year.[20] These correspond to the Christmas and New Year season of today.

3. The first known reference to December 25 as the birthday of Jesus is from 336 A.D. Prior to that, December 25 was connected to the Persian mystery cult of Mithras, whom the Romans called *Sol Invictus*, or "the invincible sun." December 25, believed to be the date the sun came to life after the winter solstice, was celebrated as the birthday of Sol Invictus.[21]

4. Roman images and writings from the time of Constantine, who had been a sun worshiper, associate Jesus with the sun god.[22] Christian leaders felt it was appropriate to associate the birthday of the physical sun with the birthday of the Sun of Righteousness (Malachi 4:2), and so December 25 began to be observed as the birthday of Christ.[23]

VII. Similarities between paganism and Christian practices.

Look at these points where Christianity began to take on the rituals and traditions of the pagan religions.

A. The practice of Lent.

In the Bible, the observance of Passover was not preceded by a ritual 40-day period of fasting or any other observance similar to Lent. The early Church did not observe this practice, and there is no scriptural basis for it.

---

20. TERTULLIAN, *On Idolatry*, chap. 14.
21. *The Encyclopedia Britannica*, (1972 ed.), s.v. "Christmas."
22. MICHAEL GRANT, *Constantine the Great* (New York: Charles Scribner's Sons, 1993), 134–136.
23. NEWMAN, vol. 1, 299.

The practice of Lent bears a resemblance to the worship of Tammuz described in Ezekiel 8:12–14. According to the legend represented in the ancient pagan festival, each year Tammuz died and was resurrected.[24] His death was observed with several weeks of weeping and fasting; then his resurrection was celebrated at the Feast of Ishtar.[25]

B.   Worship of the Queen of Heaven.

Is it God's will that we pray to Mary, the mother of Jesus, as a mediator between God and man, or honor her as a person who possessed a sinless nature from her birth?[26] The Scriptures tell us that Christ is our only Redeemer and Mediator (I Timothy 2:5). They teach us that Mary was faithful and obedient to the Lord and was "blessed among women," but they do not support the worship of Mary or prayer to anyone other than Christ. Rather, the exaltation of Mary has many similarities to the goddess worship prevalent in the ancient world up through the time of the Roman empire.

1.   Archeologists have found that some of the earliest objects of worship were images of mother and child. The Romans worshiped Cybele, originally from Asia Minor, whom they called "Great Mother." A similar goddess was Diana, or Artemis, of Ephesus (Acts 19:24–28).

---

24. JAMES GEORGE FRAZER, *The Golden Bough: A Study in Magic and Religion*, 3rd ed., pt. 4, vol. 1, *Adonis, Attis, Osirus* (New York: St. Martin's Press, 1966), 6–12.

25. JAMES HASTINGS, ed., *Encyclopedia of Religion and Ethics* (New York: Charles Scribner's Sons, 1955), s.v. "Ishtar," 433.

26. *The New Catholic Encyclopedia* (Washington, D.C.: The Catholic University of America, 1967), s.v. "Immaculate Conception."

2. The worship of a goddess who through her own virtue produces a divine offspring or causes the rebirth of a hero-god is pagan in origin. Examples of this type of worship were Cybele and Attis, Venus and Cupid, Isis and Osiris, Aphrodite and Adonis, and the Babylonian Ishtar and Tammuz.

3. Some have worshiped Mary as the "Queen of Heaven."[27] The practice of worshiping the Queen of Heaven was condemned in the Scriptures (Jeremiah 7:17–18; Jeremiah 44:15–23).

   The title "Queen of Heaven" was the name given to the Babylonian goddess Ishtar. Ishtar is probably the one referred to in the Bible as Ashtoreth,[28] the goddess who is often mentioned in connection with Israel forsaking the Lord.

   Judges 2:13   Judges 10:6   I Samuel 7:3–4
   I Samuel 12:10   I Kings 11:4–6   II Kings 23:13

C. Similarities between Roman Christianity and Buddhism.

Compare the religious practices that became part of Roman Christianity with those of Buddhism. Is there anything in the Bible that directs Christians to follow these practices?

1. These practices include image worship, masses for the dead, counting beads, chanting or meaningless repetitions of prayers, celibacy of clergy, tonsure, the practice of having monks and nuns, relic worship, systems of merit by penance, worship of saints, and Mary worship with the

---

27. HILDA GRAEF, *Mary: A History of Doctrine and Devotion,* vol. 1 (New York: Sheed and Ward, 1963), 166.
28. MCCLINTOCK AND STRONG, s.v. "Ashtoreth," 464.

Buddhist counterpart in worship of Kuan Yin, goddess of mercy.[29]

2. The first Catholic missionaries to Tibet were surprised by the similarities they saw between Tibetan practices and their own, in spite of the fact that Tibet had been isolated for many centuries.[30] Tibetan Buddhists have holy water, incense, worship of mother and child, monks, nuns, monasteries, and priestly vestments similar to the Roman Church.[31]

VIII. The destruction of mystical Babylon foretold.

The book of Revelation gives God's perspective on spiritual Babylon. It shows us God's hatred for the influence of Babylon, and it tells us how both the spirit of Babylon and its corrupting influence will be utterly destroyed. Revelation contrasts the true Bride of Christ with the harlot Babylon, both of which are described as women and as cities. The Bride, or Jerusalem from above, is described in Revelation 19:7–8 and Revelation 21:2,9–10. Babylon, the unfaithful church, is described in Revelation 17 and 18. Let's look at what Revelation tells us about the nature of Babylon.

A. Babylon is a kingdom. It is a political and economic power as well as a spiritual power.

Revelation 17:1,9–10,15,18

---

29. S.G.F. BRANDON, ed., *A Dictionary of Comparative Religion* (New York: Charles Scribner's Sons, 1970), s.v. "Images," "Dead, Prayers for the," 224, "Mass," "Rosaries," "Prayer," 507–508, "Celibacy," "Nuns," "Monasticism," "Relics," "Indulgences," "Merit," "Canonisation," "Saints," "Mercy."
30. *The Catholic Encyclopedia*, special ed. (n.p.: The Encyclopedia Press, 1913), s.v. "Buddhism (Tibetan)."
31. L. AUSTINE WADDELL, *Tibetan Buddhism* (London: W.H. Allen and Co., 1895; reprint New York: Dover Publications, Inc., 1972), 421.

B.   Babylon has corrupted the entire earth.
Revelation 17:2; 18:3; 19:2

C.   Babylon is full of blasphemy.
Revelation 17:3

D.   The colors purple and scarlet, as well as the covering of gold, precious stones, and pearls, are symbolic of Babylon's usurped religious authority.
Revelation 17:4

Aaron, who was a type of the true spiritual authority, wore garments adorned with these same decorations.
Exodus 28:4–6,15–21

E.   The blood of the saints and of all those who have been killed on the earth is found in Babylon.
Revelation 17:6   Revelation 18:24   Jeremiah 51:49

F.   Babylon has enslaved mankind and has deceived the whole earth.
Isaiah 14:4–6   Revelation 18:11,13,23

G.   God's decree is that Babylon be destroyed.
Revelation 14:8   Revelation 18:1–2,4–8,21
Jeremiah 51:29

H.   God's cry is for His people to come out of Babylon so that they do not partake of her judgments.
Revelation 18:4   Jeremiah 51:6,44–45.

IX.   **What are the harlots of Babylon?**

Babylon is the spiritual source of every abomination of the earth and the mother of harlots (Revelation 17:5). The spirit of Babylon is behind every religious system that rejects a committed relationship with the Lord and unites itself with the world. The Scriptures are filled with God's admonitions to His people not to engage in religious practices associated with idolatry. The Lord considers this to be unfaithfulness and adultery.

Exodus 34:12–17   Jeremiah 2:20–21   Ezekiel 16:15
James 4:4

The Lord wants a pure Bride, without spot or wrinkle.

Ephesians 5:25–32

X.   **The reactions caused by the destruction of mystical Babylon.**

A.   The kings of the world will destroy the harlot, the false church.

Revelation 17:16–17

B.   The political forces lament.

Revelation 18:9–10

C.   The commercial and business world laments.

Revelation 18:11–19

D.   The heavens and the saints and the apostles and prophets rejoice.

Revelation 18:20—19:9

XI.   **Satan is the spiritual power of Babylon.**

From Babel's foundation, Satan has been the real power behind Babylon. It is important to see that all the points of the Babylonian religion are a subtle counterfeit of the true.

A.   Our foe, Satan, blinds the minds of the unbeliever (II Corinthians 4:3–4), deceives with all power and lying wonders (II Thessalonians 2:9), and is our enemy (Ephesians 6:11–12).

B.   Jesus called Satan "the prince of this world" three times. Paul called him "the god of this age" and "the prince of the power of the air." His wisdom is great, for he deceives the whole world.

Revelation 12:9

C.   Satan has always sought to deceive man and corrupt his relationship with God (II Corinthians 11:3). He disguises himself as an angel of light, and his servants appear as ministers of righteousness (II Corinthians 11:13–15).

D.   Satan is the usurper and the defiler, for he seeks to defile every pure thing that God has made.

E.   Isaiah 14:3–23 associates Babylon with Lucifer, the usurper, and with demons.

F.   Babylon is the dwelling place of demons and a haunt of every foul spirit and hateful bird.

Revelation 18:2

G.   As we study Babylon with its satanic power, we realize that we have not "known the depths of Satan."

Revelation 2:24

XII. Conclusion.

In this lesson we have examined some of the influences that the spirit of Babylon has had on God's people throughout history. This teaching is not intended to single out or condemn any individual, religion, or denomination. Its purpose is to bring to our awareness areas in which our own beliefs may be affected by the deceptiveness of Satan. The Scriptures tell us that Satan is the deceiver of the whole world. Can any of us assume that we have not been tainted to some degree by the pervasive influence of Babylon? Let us look to the Holy Spirit to reveal areas where we have been hindered from a relationship with God that leads us into all the truth.

The book of Revelation begins with the Lord's entreaty, "Anyone who has an ear to hear, let him hear what the

Spirit is saying to the churches" (Revelation 2:7). God is calling His people out of Babylon and establishing His pure Bride without spot or wrinkle. These are truly days in which the Lord is restoring the purity of His Church. We must move into a pure spiritual atmosphere like that which existed in the early Church. It is only in such an atmosphere that we are able to function effectively as one Body under His Headship.

The Living Word

The Unfolding Revelation of the Word

SCRIPTURE READINGS

II Corinthians 3
John 17
I John 1:1–4

II Corinthians 4:1–11
John 1:1–18
Hebrews 8:10–13

LESSON

I.   **The created Word (by God showing His handiwork).**

Before the Bible was written, God had already revealed Himself to man by means of His creation.

Romans 1:20   Psalm 19

Compare Romans 10:18 with Psalm 19:4.

II.   **The written Word (by God speaking to man).**

A.   This revelation through the written Word came gradually through the ages. When Paul was writing his epistles to the churches, he was aware that he was anointed by God to fulfill or, more accurately, to complete the Word of God.

Colossians 1:25–26[1]

We see this also in Romans 16:25–26, New International Version: *Now to him who is able to establish you by my gospel and the proclamation of Jesus Christ, according to the revelation of the mystery hidden for long ages past, but now revealed and made known through the prophetic writings by the command of the*

---

1.   GEORGE RICKER BERRY, *The Interlinear Literal Translation of the Greek New Testament* (Grand Rapids, MI: Zondervan Publishing House, 1973).

eternal God, so that all nations might believe and obey him....

B. Paul received the deeper and more complete revelations of the Word and in a sense fulfilled the Word of God.

Ephesians 3:3–10

C. The written Word speaks to man in his own language, the language of earth and time.

III. The living Word in Jesus Christ.

A. In Jesus Christ, the Head of the Church, the revelation is glorious and full.

John 1:1–18   I John 1:1–4   Revelation 19:13

B. The created Word was not enough, and so God sent the written Word. However, that also was not enough, for "the letter kills" (II Corinthians 3:6). Then He took His Spirit and His life and wrapped them up in human flesh—"the Word was made flesh" (John 1:14).

John 6:63,68

IV. The living Word in the Body of Christ, the Church.

A. The Head of the Body is glorified, but the Body is yet to be glorified with the same glory. This must begin now in this present age.

John 17:14–24

1. The living Word began with the incarnation of Christ in human form, but it does not end there. Christ was the expression of God to man of Himself, in order that we might receive the Word in our flesh. God wants us to become the living Word also. Let the Word be made flesh in us.

2. We are to be epistles (letters) of Christ, read and known of all men.
   II Corinthians 3:2–3

3. God's Word is to be written in our minds and in our hearts.
   Hebrews 8:10

   This is the Bible that the world is to read. The Bible is written primarily to the believer, with little addressed to the unbeliever. However, as living epistles, we are to be read and known of all men.

4. The Church is the fullness of Him who fills all in all.
   Ephesians 1:23

B. God is now preparing the Church, His Body, to be His living Word to a world that gropes in darkness.
   II Corinthians 4:6–7

C. This living Word will be revealed to principalities and powers in the heavenly places.
   Ephesians 3:10 (KJV)

D. We can understand the fullness of God in Christ, but now we must begin to understand it in us.
   Hebrews 1:1–3   John 17:22–23

   1. We are His fullness and He is our fullness. We are complete in Him.
      Ephesians 1:22–23   Colossians 2:9–10

   2. We are now in the second phase of God's manifestation in the flesh, which is His manifestation in the Church. Christ is a many-membered Body.
      I Corinthians 12:12

E. The living Word: If churches would only believe that the Word is to be living and life-giving, they would no longer be concerned about oratory, eloquence, persuasive words of human wisdom, and entertainment to hold the people. Rather, they would look to God to give life to the spoken Word.

I John 1:1   John 6:63

1. As in Acts, the Word would grow, increase, and prevail.

    Acts 6:7   Acts 19:20

2. The Word is indeed God Himself spoken forth to men.

3. If we speak, let us speak as His oracles.

    I Peter 4:10–11 (KJV)

F. When this Word abides in us, and we abide in Him, then the Word in us will involve authority over nature, in judgment. It will be creative, purifying, and destructive. It will mean our enrichment, our blessing, and our fruitfulness.

John 15:7

V. **The living Word and the written Word compared.**
II Corinthians 3:1—4:11

Living Works

SCRIPTURE READINGS

Galatians 3:1–11
Hebrews 9:14
Titus 1:16
Matthew 5:13–16
Galatians 2:16
Ephesians 2:8–10

Titus 2:11–15
I Peter 2:9–12
Hebrews 6:1
Colossians 3:14–17
Titus 3:1,3–8

LESSON

I.   **What are "dead works"?**

Galatians 3:1–11

They are works that are done to earn God's favor or to be reckoned as righteousness. Dead works are our earthly, fleshly efforts to please God.

II. **We must repent of dead works.**

Hebrews 6:1   Hebrews 9:14

III. **We must leave the dead works and enter into "living works."**

Read carefully Ephesians 2:8–10 and see that we cannot be saved by our works, but by the grace of God. After we are saved, God wants us to bring forth the good works which He has ordained us to fulfill.

IV. **The inner fullness of the Spirit leads to living works and worship.**

Colossians 3:14–17

V.   **We are not to perform dead works; instead, the inner grace of God brings forth the living works in our lives.**

Titus 1:16   Titus 2:11–15   Titus 3:1,3–8
Colossians 1:28–29

VI. Living works glorify the Father because they are wrought by Christ dwelling in us.

Matthew 5:13–16   Galatians 2:20

A. God has put His light within us. It must not be hidden. Our good works must reveal the inner light and bring glory to our Father in heaven.

B. Dead works glorify man. Living works glorify the Father.

I Peter 2:9–12

Evangelism

SCRIPTURE READINGS

Acts 1:8
Acts 20:26–27
II Corinthians 4

Acts 8
Mark 16:15–18
Ezekiel 33:1–9

LESSON

I.   **In New Testament times, where did the believers witness and lead people to Christ?**

    A.   On the streets of Jerusalem and in the temple, Peter preached to the scoffers.

        Acts 2:13–14

    B.   At the temple porch, Peter witnessed to the people with miracle power.

        Acts 3:11–12   Acts 4:4

    C.   In the council chamber, the apostles boldly confessed Christ to the authorities who had crucified Him.

        Acts 5:27–29

    D.   In a chariot in the desert, Philip won the Ethiopian.

        Acts 8:29–30

    E.   In the synagogues, Paul proclaimed Jesus immediately following his conversion.

        Acts 9:20

F. In Cornelius' home, Peter preached to many and they were saved and filled with the Spirit.
Acts 10:24,44

G. At the riverside in Philippi, Paul won Lydia.
Acts 16:13–14

H. In prison, Paul and Silas led the jailer to Christ.
Acts 16:27–33

I. Paul reasoned in a school.
Acts 19:9

J. Paul taught from house to house.
Acts 20:20

K. In jail, Paul spoke to Felix of the faith.
Acts 24:23–24

L. In court before King Agrippa, Paul testified.
Acts 26:1

M. In custody waiting for trial, Paul preached and taught.
Acts 28:16,30–31

II. **In New Testament times, how did the believers bring people into a relationship with Christ?**

Let us consider the deacon Philip, who became a great evangelist.
Acts 8

A. Philip obeyed the Spirit's leading.
Verses 29–30

B. He listened to the eunuch's questions (the eunuch had a prepared heart).
Verses 30–35

A ready Word from God for a ready heart that God has prepared—this is the formula for evangelism today.

C.   He began with a direct question.
     Verse 30

D.   He used the Word of God.
     Verse 35

E.   He presented Jesus Christ (not a doctrine, a denomination, or a church).
     Verse 35

F.   He followed through.
     Verses 36–38

G.   He was filled with the Spirit (Acts 6:3). He was obedient (verse 27). He was earnest (verse 30). He exalted the Lord (verse 35).

III.   **Why should all believers bring people into a relationship with Christ?**

A.   To deliver ourselves from the blood of all men.
     Acts 20:26–27   Ezekiel 33:6

B.   To be faithful stewards of what God has given us.
     I Corinthians 4:1–5

C.   To be His witnesses unto the ends of the earth, as He commanded us.
     Acts 1:8

     We have received an anointing of the Lord. We must not use this anointing just to minister to one another; it is given to do a work. It is time to carry the Word of God to those who need it.

IV. **Here is a picture of the New Testament ministry.**

II Corinthians 4

See what is wrought **within** the vessel. See what is wrought **through** the vessel.

V. **The signs and miracles will follow us when we faithfully declare the Word that the Lord has put within us.**

Mark 16:15–18

The Consecrated Life

SCRIPTURE READINGS

Joel 2:12–17, 28–29
Galatians 6:14–16
II Peter 2:9–22
Romans 1

II Thessalonians 2:8–14
Philippians 3:8–21
I Corinthians 1, 3, 5, 6, and 11

LESSON

I. **The gifts of the Holy Spirit may coexist with a carnal self-life.**

    A. The first epistle to the Corinthians was written because the self-life and the Holy Spirit were both in evidence in the believers in that church. This condition should not be.

    B. All the gifts and ministries of the Holy Spirit, including spiritual wisdom and revelation, were found in the Corinthian church, yet the fleshly carnal nature was present also.

    I Corinthians 1:4–13

        1. They exalted worldly wisdom and were guilty of man-worship.

        I Corinthians 1:10–31

        2. There was carnal division and immaturity among the believers.

        I Corinthians 3:1–6

        3. There was gross immorality.

        I Corinthians 5

4. There was litigation against other believers.
   I Corinthians 6:1–8

5. There was sensuality.
   I Corinthians 6:9–20

6. There was intemperance.
   I Corinthians 11:20–22

II. **What was the cause of this condition?**

A. They lacked a deep consecration to live for God. There was no experience of the cross of Christ in their lives. Paul said that such are enemies of the cross of Christ.
   Philippians 3:8–21

B. The lack of a cross experience means the lack of a ministry to the world of the life of Christ.
   Galatians 6:14–16   Galatians 2:20–21

III. **There is a difference between being delivered from sin and demon oppression and being consecrated to live for God.**

You may be delivered from sin and Satan, or from evil spirits, and still not really desire to put away the self-life and serve God. Many are truly delivered; however, when they face temptation again, they fall and are overcome again because there is no real dedication in them to do the will of God and to serve Him. You will either serve self or serve the Lord.

IV. **What will happen to us if we are repeatedly delivered from sin and demon oppression and we do not dedicate ourselves to really serve God?**

   A.   The latter state is worse than the first, for a worse thing will come upon us. We have turned the grace of God into lasciviousness.

   Jude 3–4   II Peter 2:9–22

   B.   We dare not hold the truth without walking in it, for the wrath of God comes against those who hold the truth in unrighteousness.

   Romans 1:16–18,21–32

V. **What will happen to those who will not accept the Word that God is speaking and walk in it?**

   II Thessalonians 2:8–14

   They will receive strong delusions to believe the false, that they might be judged.

The Cross

SCRIPTURE READINGS

Galatians 2:16–21
Galatians 5:13–26
Philippians 2:5–11
Hebrews 2:9–18
Hebrews 12:1–3
Romans 6:6
Galatians 6:12–16
Philippians 3:7–21
Hebrews 9:13–28

Hebrews 8:8–13
Colossians 1:15–22
II Corinthians 4:11–12
Galatians 3:1–14,29
Ephesians 2:11–22
Colossians 2:9–23
Hebrews 10:5–25
I Corinthians 1:17–25
II Timothy 2:11

LESSON

I.   **Why is the cross important to us?**

The preaching of the cross is the power of God.

I Corinthians 1:17–18

II. **What did the Lord Jesus Christ accomplish on His cross?**

A.   On His cross, Christ reconciled us—even the whole universe—to God.

Colossians 1:15–22

B.   On His cross, Christ abolished the law of commandments and ordinances and reconciled both Israel and the Gentiles to God.

Ephesians 2:11–22

C.   On His cross, Christ canceled the demands of the Law against us; He disarmed and defeated principalities and powers (Satan); He brought us to fullness of life, having forgiven all our trespasses.

Colossians 2:9–23

D. On His cross, Christ tasted death for every man, that He might destroy him who has the power of death (Satan) and deliver us from the fear of death.

Hebrews 2:9–18

E. By His death on His cross, a new "testament" or will is in effect for us.

Hebrews 9:13–28

This new testament or covenant is given in Hebrews 8:8–13.

F. On His cross, Christ offered the perfect and final sacrifice for sins, and by a single sacrifice He has perfected for all time those who are sanctified.

Hebrews 10:5–25

III. **What does the cross of Jesus Christ mean to us?**

A. Through His cross, Christ brings a new life to us— the Christ-life.

Galatians 2:16–21

B. Through His cross, Christ brings the blessings and the covenant of Abraham to us.

Galatians 3:1–14,29

C. Through His cross, we can see the flesh, with its passions and lusts, crucified.

Galatians 5:13–26

D. Through His cross, we can be crucified to the world, and the world crucified to us. This is our "circumcision."

Galatians 6:12–16

What great spiritual results are wrought in us by the cross of Christ!

IV. **What is the process by which all these things become an actual experience to us?**

Romans 6:6   II Corinthians 4:11–12   Galatians 4:19
Galatians 2:20   II Timothy 2:11

A. In Philippians 3:7–21, we see that the enemies of the cross of Christ are those who refuse to let the victory of the cross be worked in them. They would rather follow their carnal appetites.

B. We must submit to this work of the cross in us.
Matthew 16:24–25

Waiting on the Lord

LESSON

45

SCRIPTURE READINGS

Isaiah 30:15–21
I Corinthians 2:9–13
Luke 10:38–42
Isaiah 64:4

Habakkuk 2:2–4
Isaiah 40:27–31
Romans 8:19,23,25

LESSON

I. **What is "waiting on the Lord"?**

It is active faith which seeks direction, revelation, and sustenance from the Lord, that His life and will might be manifested in us. It means the renouncing of our wills and decisions in order to wait for the revelation of His will in our lives.

II. **Waiting at the feet of the Lord is the one needful thing for all of us.**

Luke 10:38–42

A. The Marthas are always critical, very religious, very busy, statistically successful, anxious for many things.

B. The Marys are sacrificing many good things for the best things. Their emphasis is on the best.

What is the important and needful thing for you?

C. Waiting on the Lord is not an added luxury to a life filled with our own ways and activities. Waiting on the Lord is the basis of a Spirit-directed and Christ-empowered life. If you are ineffective and going in circles, wait on the Lord.

D. Most believers need to be delivered from the oppression of the cares and pressures of life. They need to wait on the Lord with fasting and prayer until they receive the assurance of His will and His strength.

III. **Strength and endurance come through waiting on the Lord.**

Isaiah 40:27–31

The Hebrew word *qavah*, translated "to wait," means "to wait, expect, look for."

IV. **Waiting on the Lord will bring things into your life beyond your capacity to comprehend.**

Isaiah 64:4, quoted in I Corinthians 2:9–13

The Hebrew word used in Isaiah 64:4 is *chakah*, which means "to wait earnestly."

V. **Waiting on the Lord brings the guidance and direction that you will need.**

Isaiah 30:15–21

The Hebrew word used in verse 18 is also *chakah*.

VI. **Hasty decision and action is behind every failure.**

Proverbs 19:2   Proverbs 29:20

Let us be quick to hear, slow to speak, slow to wrath.
James 1:19

VII. **We are especially commanded to wait on the Lord in this end time.**

Habakkuk 2:2–4   Zephaniah 3:8–9,16–20   Luke 12:36
Romans 8:19,23,25

VIII. **In waiting on the Lord, we may receive the mind of the Lord and forsake our own way, that we may humbly fulfill His will.**

Philippians 2:1–16

Entering into God's Rest

SCRIPTURE READINGS

Hebrews 3 and 4

LESSON

I. **God made a promise of His rest.**
   Hebrews 4:9

II. **These are the factors which prevent your entering into His rest.**

   A. Hardening your heart.
      Hebrews 3:8,13,15   Hebrews 4:7

   B. Unbelief.
      Hebrews 3:19

   C. Disobedience.
      Hebrews 3:18   Hebrews 4:6,11

III. **Israel never entered into God's rest.**

   A. Israel missed it in the wilderness because of rebellion, unbelief, and hardened hearts.
      Hebrews 3:7–11,16–19

   B. Israel missed it under Joshua.
      Hebrews 4:8

   C. Israel still did not have it in David's day.
      Hebrews 4:7

IV. The promise of a Sabbath rest for the people of God is still standing.

Hebrews 4:9   Hebrews 4:6

V. It is God's rest.

Hebrews 4:3–4,10

A. "All His works were finished from the foundation of the world" (verse 3). Entering into His rest means the end of our labors, as it did with God.

B. His rest is a spiritual rest, not a natural rest. It means the end of fleshly striving and zeal and the beginning of living and ministering by His fullness and by His victory, rather than by our labors.

VI. We strive to enter His rest.

Hebrews 4:11

We strive to enter His rest so that we do not fall by following the same example of unbelief and disobedience as those who sinned in the wilderness.

VII. What is the means of bringing us into His rest?

The living Word of God.

A. When we hear His voice, we must not harden our hearts.

Hebrews 3:7–11

B. The Word they heard did not benefit them, because it was not believed.

Hebrews 4:1–3

C. What the Word of God does.

Hebrews 4:11–12

1. The Word cuts us deep, because entering into His rest is a spiritual process. The Word works the spiritual inner preparation that brings us

into His rest. The picture used is that of the knife which prepares the Levitical sacrifice upon the altar of God.

2. The Word is living and active.

D. The Word comes line upon line, precept upon precept, and this is the rest. The babes hear the Word; some reject it, stumble backward, and are snared and taken captive. Let us hear and enter into His rest.

Isaiah 28:9–13

REVIEW QUESTIONS

1. Can you explain how the promise of rest remains standing even though those to whom it was originally given were never able to enter into it?

2. What prevents God's people from entering into His rest?

3. Why is this rest most needed today?

The Latter Rain

SCRIPTURE READINGS

Joel 2 and 3   Acts 2
Zechariah 10:1   James 5:7–8
Hosea 6:1–3   Isaiah 44:3–4

LESSON

I.   **The vineyard of Joel.**

The Old Testament prophet Joel pictures a vineyard destroyed by insects; but the vineyard is restored by the rains that God sends upon it. It is a picture of God pouring out His Spirit on a weak and dying Church so that it might be restored.

Joel 1:1–20   Joel 2:23–32

A.   In the mid-season, the latter rain is promised. This is the pre-harvest rain that is needed to mature the crops.

Joel 2:23

B.   Plenty is promised.

Joel 2:24,26

C.   A restoration of what the insects have destroyed of the vineyard is promised.

Joel 1:4   Joel 2:25

D.   God's people will have abundance and will never be ashamed.

Joel 2:26–27

E. The "outpouring on all flesh" means that the latter rain of the Holy Spirit will fall on all of God's people, with the supernatural in evidence—visions and prophesyings.
Joel 2:28–29

F. After that will follow the signs which precede the day of the Lord.
Joel 2:30–32

II. **The meaning and significance of this picture.**

A. What is the meaning of the vineyard or the garden?

It is God's people.
I Corinthians 3:6–9

B. What is the meaning of the insects?

Satan is the devourer.
I Peter 5:8

C. What is the meaning of the latter rain?

It is the outpouring of God's Spirit.
Acts 2:14–21

D. When is this outpouring of the Spirit to take place?

It will take place in the last days.
Joel 2:28

This verse in Joel reads "afterward," or "after this." When it is quoted in Acts 2:17, it reads "in the last days."

E. Is this outpouring of the Spirit now past?

No. We have not yet seen all the signs of the tribulation that were prophesied, nor have we seen the level of deliverance that Joel spoke of.
Joel 2:30–32

      1.   Also, James prophesied that the latter rain
would come just prior to the return of the Lord.

         James 5:7–8

      2.   The primary purpose of this latter rain of the
Spirit is to prepare God's people for the return of
the Lord.

F.   Is this outpouring of the Spirit for Israel only?

The promise of the Spirit is for as many as the Lord
shall call.

Acts 2:16,38–39

God Confirms His Word

The Law of Witness

SCRIPTURE READINGS

Hebrews 2:1–4
Deuteronomy 19:15
II Corinthians 13:1
I Corinthians 14:37–40
Mark 16:15–20
Deuteronomy 17:6

I Timothy 5:19
Hebrews 10:28–31
Numbers 35:30
Matthew 18:15–22
I Corinthians 14:20–33

LESSON

I. **God's Word delivered by angels was steadfast and confirmed.**

    Hebrews 2:1–2

II. **God's Word delivered by the disciples was confirmed.**

    Hebrews 2:3–4   Mark 16:15–20

    The element of spirit and life in the living Word of God always results in signs and miracles. These things are God's confirmation of His Word.

III. **The law of witness: every Word of God is confirmed by two or three witnesses.**

    Let us trace this principle in the Scriptures.

    A. The law of witness in the Old Testament.
        Deuteronomy 19:15   Deuteronomy 17:6
        Numbers 35:30

B. The law of witness in the New Testament.
Matthew 18:15–22   II Corinthians 13:1
I Timothy 5:19

    1.   Note that Jesus sent the disciples out two by two.
        Mark 6:7

    2.   Then the seventy were also sent out two by two.
        Luke 10:1

Thus, God confirms the message with two or three witnesses.

C. Does God always hold to the two or three witnesses? Apparently.

    1.   The Ark of the Covenant—two cherubim to witness the blood.
        Exodus 25:17–21

    2.   Two of twelve spies were witnesses against Israel's unbelief; for this God preserved them.
        Numbers 14:6–9,36–38

    3.   There were two witnesses to Mary's conception— Joseph and Elizabeth. There were also angels.
        Matthew 1:18–25   Luke 1:41–45

    4.   Two thieves were witnesses to Jesus' death.
        Matthew 27:38

    5.   Two angels were witnesses to His resurrection and to His ascension.
        Luke 24:1–7   Acts 1:9–11

    6.   Two witnesses were present at the transfiguration.
        Luke 9:30–31

7. There are three witnesses in heaven and three witnesses on earth.

I John 5:6–10 (KJV)

IV. **Two or three witnesses are required in the Body of Christ—that is, in the ministry to the church.**

I Corinthians 14:20–33,37–40

A. In I Corinthians 14:27, tongues are limited to two or at the most three, and they must be interpreted. Why is this limitation imposed? God has His twofold witness by one tongue and one interpretation.

B. In I Corinthians 14:29, we see that at least two or three prophets should speak. This refers to revelation prophecy (verse 30). All may prophesy (verses 24,31), but not all have the prophetic office to move as a prophet in revelation. Why must at least two or three prophets speak? On any matter as important as revelation over an individual, God gives two or three witnesses to establish every Word. Even when two or three prophets speak, each of the other prophets is still to judge carefully what is said (verse 29).

Note: Prophesying gifts and ministries over an individual is specifically a function of a foundational ministry. Those who do not have the office of a prophet or an apostle should participate in this only when under the authority of a prophet or an apostle.

C. Why does God want two or three witnesses to what He imparts to us?

1. God wants sufficient witness so we can be certain of His gift and purposes for us.

2. God also wants sufficient witness of the giving of His talents or gifts, so that He might require them of us. With two or three witnesses, we have no excuse in the day of judgment.
Hebrews 10:28–31

D. If you do not have the proper office or calling, do not try to minister revelation unless under the proper authority in the church. God has an order, and He does not want confusion.
I Corinthians 14:33,40

   1. See God's judgment on those who usurp an office which is not theirs.

      a. On King Saul, for moving as a priest.
         I Samuel 13:5–14

      b. On Korah, for usurping the authority of Moses.
         Numbers 16

      c. On Miriam, for murmuring against Moses.
         Numbers 12

      d. On angels that left their domain (or sphere).
         Jude 6,8–11

      e. On Simon, for coveting the apostolic office.
         Acts 8:18–24

      Don't overshoot your bounds.
      Romans 12:3

2. Your gift is unlimited, and your ministry is unlimited, when you move within the divine limits set for you. Avoid ministering by yourself as much as possible when it goes beyond edification, exhortation, and comfort. Beyond this, Body ministry is the way. What we do, we must do as a Body. We must be united in spirit, in vision, and in ministry.

REVIEW QUESTIONS

1. Explain the law of witness in your own words.

2. Name as many instances as you can where this law of witness worked in the Old Testament. Do the same for the New Testament.

3. Explain I Corinthians 14:27,29. Why is it that two or three prophets are to speak?

Impartation

SCRIPTURE READINGS

I Timothy
II Timothy

INTRODUCTION

From the beginning, God has perpetuated what He is doing within His people by enabling them to impart that inner divine deposit in a measure to others. The Old Testament patriarchs imparted to their children by prophecy and blessing and laying on of hands. The prophets commissioned and imparted abilities by laying on of hands and also by prophetic Word. The Old Testament priesthood was set apart and enabled by such impartation.

In the New Testament, impartation and appropriation followed the same Old Testament patterns. We see also that in the ordinances of the Church, impartation and appropriation are intended in each observance:

- Water baptism.

- The Lord's Supper.

- Anointing the sick with oil.

- Laying hands on elders and other ministries to ordain them.

- Foot washing.

The Scriptures given below are basic in the teaching of New Testament impartation and appropriation.

Caution: You cannot impart a measure of Christ that you have not appropriated yourself. You cannot give the spiritual reality of Christ to others if you do not have it yourself.

LESSON

I.   **Impartation and appropriation by prophecy.**
      I Timothy 1:18–20

II.   **Impartation and appropriation by careful study of the Scriptures.**

      ...nourishing thyself with the words of the faith and of the noble teaching which thou hast closely studied. But from the profane and old-wives' stories excuse thyself, and be training thyself unto godliness. I Timothy 4:6–7, The Emphasized Bible, by Joseph Rotherham.

III. **Impartation by the elders (prophecy and laying on of hands).**
      I Timothy 4:11–14

IV.   **Impartation by diligence.**

      By taking heed to himself and to the teaching, Timothy and his hearers grew.
      I Timothy 4:15–16

      A caution is given in I Timothy 5:22. Timothy was not to lay hands suddenly on another. Why? Premature impartation (as in ordaining elders) leads to premature trials and often failure.

V.   **Parental impartation.**
      II Timothy 1:3–5

VI.   **Apostolic impartation (the laying on of hands).**
      II Timothy 1:6–7

VII. **Teaching impartation (the living Word).**
      II Timothy 1:12–13   II Timothy 2:2–3

      An outline have thou of healthful discourses which from me thou hast heard.... II Timothy 1:13, The Emphasized Bible.

"These things entrust to faithful men." II Timothy 2:2–3. Note the sufferings and testings involved.

VIII. Impartation by speaking the living Word of God.

    A.   II Timothy 2:8–18

        Verse 10 speaks of salvation and age-abiding glory. Verses 14–16 call for us to rightly handle the Word, and *...not to be waging word-battles, useful for nothing....* Verse 14, The Emphasized Bible.

    B.   II Timothy 3:10—4:5

        The living Word is a growing and developing thing in us. This passage opens up another great truth: some cannot endure the living Word. It shakes them and they turn away from it.

IX.   The basic law of impartation: like begets like.
Matthew 7:15–20

That born of the flesh is fleshly (John 3:6); that born of the soul is soulish; that born of the Spirit is spiritual. The river does not rise above its source. There can be great development within a species, but one species does not develop into another. We read in Genesis 1:20–25 that God created all life to bring forth after its kind. This is true also of the spiritual realm.

The Three Great Steps in the Perfection of the Church

(An Exposition of I Corinthians 12 and 13)

SCRIPTURE READINGS

I Corinthians 12 and 13

INTRODUCTION

Every spiritual movement in the past has been characterized by the presumption of men that everything God had for them was conveyed in the single fresh experience that they received from God.

- Many fundamentalist groups teach that when a new believer accepts Christ, he is baptized by the Holy Spirit and receives "everything."

- The Holiness movement claimed that their experience brought them everything: the baptism of the Holy Spirit, sanctification, and the eradication of the sin nature.

- The early recipients of the Pentecostal experience believed that they had a final and complete experience in God when they received the Holy Spirit and spoke in tongues.

- The Latter Rain movement claimed to be walking in the ministry of the Body of Christ, including the restored foundational ministries, when they actually had received only a beginning of the gifts of the Holy Spirit.

Presumption leads us to claim too much, while unbelief leads us to claim too little. Faith brings a sober estimate: *For through the grace given to me I say to every man among you not to think more highly of himself than he ought to think; but to think so as to have sound judgment, as God has allotted to each a measure of faith.* Romans 12:3.

As we study this lesson, we will see that there are three phases in our perfection in God as believers. We will also see that most of us are only in the process of the first phase. This lesson should crush spiritual pride, where we think we have all that God has for us; and it should encourage us to see that God has much for us that is yet to be revealed.

LESSON

I.   **There are three steps or phases in our perfection in God.**

These are identified in I Corinthians 12:1–7.

A.   Diversities of gifts by the same Spirit (the Holy Spirit).
Verse 4

B.   Diversities of ministries by the same Lord (Jesus Christ).
Verse 5

C.   Diversities of operations (or effects, NASB) by the same God (the Father). The Greek word for operations is *energema*, which means "energies."
Verse 6

This would indicate that first we come into the gifts of the Holy Spirit; then we grow or develop in the Lord Jesus Christ into a ministry as a member of the Body of Christ; and finally, we are indwelt by the fullness of God unto the release of His great energizing or operations through us.

II. These three phases through which we must all pass as God brings us into perfection in these last days are described in the twelfth and thirteenth chapters of I Corinthians.

A. Different gifts of the Holy Spirit.

I Corinthians 12:4   I Corinthians 12:7–11

B. Different ministries in the Body of Christ.

I Corinthians 12:5   I Corinthians 12:11–31

C. Different operations or energies released by the fullness of God within the perfected believer.

I Corinthians 12:6   I Corinthians 13

I Corinthians 13 shows the way into this last great step.

1. Verses 1–3 show that we are yet nothing without His love.

2. Verses 4–7 show what we become by the release of God's love within us.

3. Verses 8–13 show that **this love is the fullness** of which the former steps are only a part.

D. I Corinthians 13:13 is the summation of chapters 12 and 13.

1. Faith: the key to the gifts of the Holy Spirit.

2. Hope: the key to the fullness of the Body of Christ.

3. Love: the key to the coming fullness of God within us.

    E.   These three steps show us what we are becoming as we walk on with God.

        Step 1. The endowments that rest upon us **by the Spirit in us**.

        Step 2. What we are becoming in relation to the Lord, **in Christ the Head of the Body**.

        Step 3. What God will become in us, **God in us**.

III.   **The same order is given in John 14:14–23 and Ephesians 3:14–21, where our unfolding spiritual development is described again in these same three phases.**

IV.   **What step are we in at present?**

    Most Spirit-filled believers who have been moving on with God are in the first step. Some have entered into the second step. But most of us have not even comprehended the smallest part of what God has in store for us.

REVIEW QUESTIONS

1.   How many of the gifts of the Holy Spirit can you name?

2.   How many of the ministries in the Body of Christ can you name?

3.   Do you think that each step involves definite experiences for the believer?

4.   Read and discuss the epilogue, "Three Steps to Our Perfection."

Three Steps to Our Perfection

One of the greatest revelations to come in the ministry of the living Word is given in Lesson 50 of this manual, "The Three Great Steps in the Perfection of the Church." This lesson is the conclusion to all of the teaching presented in this manual. As important as this teaching is, it has been the least understood. Lesson 50 is a very simple outline of the steps to our perfection in God, which involve three different phases of experience that come to the individual. Many people have taught that this has already happened; however, God gave this teaching prophetically in preparation for what is to come. In John 14, Jesus talks about the Holy Spirit coming to abide within the individual believer. He says that He also will come and manifest Himself to us. He then goes on to say, "My Father and I will take up Our abode in you" (verses 16–18,21,23). This is our goal.

Ephesians 3 talks about our being filled with the Holy Spirit; but much more than that, it speaks of our being filled with all the fullness of God (verses 16–19). As Christ was in this world and in Him dwelt all the fullness of the Godhead bodily (Colossians 2:9), so also the design for every person who comes into Christ is to go through the successive experiences until the fullness of God dwells in him too. This experience is clearly outlined in the Scriptures. It is such a beautiful thing.

We read in the Scriptures, "The Spirit spoke," yet we know that the Word was coming through human channels (II Samuel 23:2; II Peter 1:21). Paul spoke about the anointing that was upon him and the challenge of the Corinthian church in seeking proof of Christ's speaking in him (II Corinthians 13:3). In Galatians 2:20, Paul talked about Christ living in him. This was the reality of Paul's life. Oh, how glibly some Christians have mouthed those same words. If they only knew the truth!

I know that Paul said, *But if any man hath not the Spirit of Christ, he is none of his.* Romans 8:9b, ASV. But he also said, *I am crucified with Christ: nevertheless I live; yet not I, but Christ liveth in me: and the life which I now live in the flesh I live by the faith of the Son of God, who loved me, and gave himself for me. I do not frustrate the grace of God.* Galatians 2:20–21a, KJV. He was talking about a fantastic thing—not some theory, but an actual, living experience.

When we speak about a Spirit-filled life, we mean it. When we talk about Christ coming forth in an individual, we mean it. And when we talk about the fullness of the Father, we mean that too. His fullness is a promise that belongs to the obedient ones. Jesus said, "If you obey Me, if you keep My commandments, if you keep My Word, My Father will love you, and We will take up Our abode in you" (John 14:23).

Read Lesson 50 again. Study it carefully, and every Scripture in it, because I believe there is an urgency of the Holy Spirit to talk to us about the perfection of the human spirit. I believe that this is the time when He is leading us into this third great plane of experience. I do not think anyone has touched it yet. Some have looked at it, approached it, and received foreshadows of it; but now it is coming.

Are you open to the things in the Word of God which are yet to come? Do you believe that there are more truths hidden right in plain sight in the Bible than anyone has walked in? Many truths are hidden there, waiting for the Spirit to reveal them to those blessed ones who have ears to hear.

The Eternal Worship of God Described in the Book of Revelation

This appendix is referenced in Lesson 18.

Revelation 4:8–9	The four living creatures do not cease to worship day and night.
Revelation 4:10–11	The twenty-four elders fall down and worship before Him who sits on the throne.
Revelation 5:8–10	The four living creatures and the twenty-four elders fall down before the Lamb and sing a new song.
Revelation 5:11–12	The four living creatures, the twenty-four elders, and all the angels worship.
Revelation 5:13	Every created thing—in heaven and on earth and under the earth and on the sea—worships.
Revelation 5:14	The living creatures and the elders worship.
Revelation 11:16–18	The twenty-four elders fall on their faces and worship God.
Revelation 14:1–3	The one hundred and forty-four thousand who are purchased from the earth sing a new song before the throne.

Revelation 15:2–4	Those who are victorious from the beast sing the song of Moses and of the Lamb.
Revelation 19:1–2	The multitude in heaven worship a first time.
Revelation 19:3	The multitude in heaven worship a second time.
Revelation 19:4	The elders and the living creatures worship God.
Revelation 19:5	A voice from the throne commands the bond servants to worship.
Revelation 19:6–8	The great multitude, like the sound of many waters and mighty peals of thunder, worship and rejoice over the marriage of the Lamb.

Healings Recorded in the Book of Luke

This appendix is referenced in Lesson 22.

Luke 1:64	Zacharias' mouth was opened and his tongue loosed.
Luke 4:33–35	The man possessed by a demon was healed when Jesus rebuked the demon.
Luke 4:38–39	Simon's mother was healed when Jesus rebuked the fever.
Luke 4:40–41	Many were healed by the laying on of hands.
Luke 5:12–13	The leper was healed when Jesus touched him.
Luke 5:15	Great multitudes were healed.
Luke 5:18–25	The paralyzed man was healed when Jesus told him to get up and go home.
Luke 6:6–10	A man with a withered hand was healed when Jesus told him to stretch out his hand.
Luke 6:18–19	The whole multitude sought to touch Him—power coming from Him healed them all.
Luke 7:2–10	The centurion's slave was healed by a Word (Matthew 8:8,13).

Luke 7:12–15	The widow's son was raised from the dead by a command.
Luke 7:21–22	Many were healed, including the blind, lame, lepers, and deaf; the dead were brought back to life.
Luke 8:2–3	Various women were healed of evil spirits and sicknesses, including Mary Magdalene "from whom seven demons had gone out."
Luke 8:27–33	The man possessed by many demons was made well by a command.
Luke 8:43–44	The woman with a hemorrhage was healed by touching Jesus.
Luke 8:41–42,49–56	Jairus' daughter was raised from the dead when Jesus took her by the hand and spoke to her.
Luke 9:11	Jesus cured those who had need of healing.
Luke 9:38–42	The boy with convulsions was healed when Jesus rebuked the unclean spirit.
Luke 11:14	The man possessed by a demon was able to speak after Jesus cast out the demon.
Luke 13:11–14	The woman who for 18 years had an illness caused by a spirit was healed on the Sabbath by Jesus speaking to her and laying hands on her.
Luke 14:2–4	Jesus took hold of the man with dropsy (edema) and healed him.

Luke 17:11–14	Ten lepers were healed by a command.
Luke 18:35–43	The blind man was healed by a Word.
Luke 22:50–51	The ear of the high priest's slave was healed by a touch.

Scriptural Names for Satan

This appendix is referenced in Lesson 24.

Revelation 9:11	Apollyon and Abaddon
Revelation 12:10	The accuser of the brethren
I Peter 5:8	The adversary
II Corinthians 6:15	Belial
Matthew 12:24,26	Beelzebub
Revelation 12:9	The Devil
II Corinthians 4:4	The god of this world (or age)
Ephesians 2:2	The prince of the power of the air
John 12:31	The ruler (prince, KJV) of this world
Revelation 20:2	The serpent
I John 5:18	The wicked one

Different Natures and Personalities of Demonic Spirits

This appendix is referenced in Lesson 24.

I Samuel 28:7 (KJV)	Familiar spirit (used by a medium)
Numbers 5:14	Spirit of jealousy
I Samuel 16:23	Evil spirit
I Samuel 1:2–10,13–16 (KJV)	Sorrowful spirit
I Kings 22:22	Lying spirit
Proverbs 16:18	Haughty spirit
Isaiah 19:14 (KJV)	Perverse spirit
Isaiah 29:10	Spirit of deep sleep
Isaiah 61:3	Spirit of heaviness
Hosea 4:12	Spirit of harlotry
Zechariah 13:2	Unclean spirit

Matthew 12:45	Wicked spirit
I Timothy 4:1 (KJV)	Seducing spirit
Mark 9:17	Mute spirit
Mark 9:25	Deaf spirit
Revelation 18:2 (KJV)	Foul spirit
Luke 13:11	Spirit of infirmity
Romans 8:15	Spirit of bondage
Romans 11:8	Spirit of slumber
I John 4:3	Spirit of antichrist
I John 4:6	Spirit of error
Revelation 16:14 (NASB)	Spirit of demons
II Samuel 6:14–23 Mark 3:1-6	Spirit of criticism
Numbers 16 Ephesians 2:2	Rebellious spirit
II Timothy 1:7	Spirit of fear
Habakkuk 1:3 I Corinthians 3:3	Spirit of strife and division

Scriptural References to Jesus as Savior

Lesson 31 points out that Jesus is called Savior sixteen times in the New Testament, while He is called Lord seven hundred times. The references to His Lordship are found abundantly throughout the New Testament and are too numerous to list here. The sixteen references to Jesus as our Savior are provided below; all of the quotations are taken from the New American Standard Bible.

Luke 2:10–11	*And the angel said to them, "Do not be afraid; for behold, I bring you good news of a great joy which shall be for all the people; for today in the city of David there has been born for you a Savior, who is Christ the Lord."*
John 4:39–42	*And from that city many of the Samaritans believed in Him because of the word of the woman who testified, "He told me all the things that I have done." So when the Samaritans came to Him, they were asking Him to stay with them; and He stayed there two days. And many more believed because of His word; and they were saying to the woman, "It is no longer because of what you said that we believe, for we have heard for ourselves and know that this One is indeed the Savior of the world."*

Acts 5:30–31	*"The God of our fathers raised up Jesus, whom you had put to death by hanging Him on a cross. He is the one whom God exalted to His right hand as a Prince and a Savior, to grant repentance to Israel, and forgiveness of sins."*
Acts 13:23	*"From the offspring of this man, according to promise, God has brought to Israel a Savior, Jesus."*
Ephesians 5:23	*For the husband is the head of the wife, as Christ also is the head of the church, He Himself being the Savior of the body.*
Philippians 3:20–21	*For our citizenship is in heaven, from which also we eagerly wait for a Savior, the Lord Jesus Christ; who will transform the body of our humble state into conformity with the body of His glory, by the exertion of the power that He has even to subject all things to Himself.*
II Timothy 1:8–10	*Therefore do not be ashamed of the testimony of our Lord, or of me His prisoner; but join with me in suffering for the gospel according to the power of God, who has saved us, and called us with a holy calling, not according to our works, but according to His own purpose and grace which was granted us in Christ Jesus from all eternity, but now has been revealed by the appearing of our Savior Christ Jesus, who abolished death, and brought life and immortality to light through the gospel.*
Titus 1:4	*To Titus, my true child in a common faith: Grace and peace from God the Father and Christ Jesus our Savior.*

Titus 2:11–14	*For the grace of God has appeared, bringing salvation to all men, instructing us to deny ungodliness and worldly desires and to live sensibly, righteously and godly in the present age, looking for the blessed hope and the appearing of the glory of our great God and Savior, Christ Jesus; who gave Himself for us, that He might redeem us from every lawless deed and purify for Himself a people for His own possession, zealous for good deeds.*
Titus 3:4–7	*But when the kindness of God our Savior and His love for mankind appeared, He saved us, not on the basis of deeds which we have done in righteousness, but according to His mercy, by the washing of regeneration and renewing by the Holy Spirit, whom He poured out upon us richly through Jesus Christ our Savior, that being justified by His grace we might be made heirs according to the hope of eternal life.*
II Peter 1:1	*Simon Peter, a bond-servant and apostle of Jesus Christ, to those who have received a faith of the same kind as ours, by the righteousness of our God and Savior, Jesus Christ.*
II Peter 1:11	*For in this way the entrance into the eternal kingdom of our Lord and Savior Jesus Christ will be abundantly supplied to you.*

II Peter 2:20	*For if after they have escaped the defilements of the world by the knowledge of the Lord and Savior Jesus Christ, they are again entangled in them and are overcome, the last state has become worse for them than the first.*
II Peter 3:1–2	*This is now, beloved, the second letter I am writing to you in which I am stirring up your sincere mind by way of reminder, that you should remember the words spoken beforehand by the holy prophets and the commandment of the Lord and Savior spoken by your apostles.*
II Peter 3:18	*But grow in the grace and knowledge of our Lord and Savior Jesus Christ. To Him be the glory, both now and to the day of eternity. Amen.*
I John 4:14	*And we have beheld and bear witness that the Father has sent the Son to be the Savior of the world.*